Planted in Love

The Enneagram
Reasoning and Conversion

ST PAULS

ST PAULS
Middlegreen, Slough SL3 6BT, United Kingdom
Moyglare Road, Maynooth, Co. Kildare, Ireland

© Elizabeth McNulty 1995

Cover design by Sr Marie Louis De Monfor

ISBN 085439 502 4

Set by TuKan, High Wycombe
Printed by The Guernsey Press Co. Ltd, Guernsey, C.I.

ST PAULS is an activity of the priests and brothers of the
Society of St Paul who proclaim the Gospel through the media of
social communication

Contents

'Out of his infinite glory,
may he give you the power through his Spirit
for your hidden self to grow strong,
so that Christ may live in your hearts through faith,
and then
Planted in Love
and
Built on Love
you will, with all the Saints,
have the strength to grasp the breadth and the length
the height and the depth until,
knowing the love of Christ which is beyond all knowledge,
you are filled with the utter fullness of God'
(Eph 3:14-19).

ACKNOWLEDGEMENTS

This book has been in the writing for almost five years, and the fact that it is now published is due to the help and encouragement of many kind friends and colleagues.

I wish especially to thank Sr Mary Bonaventure and Br Charles Gay who being the first to see the manuscript were generous with comments and encouragement. I thank Sr Carmel Looby, my provincial superior, for her confidence in my ability to complete the project and Sr Bernadette Judge who put her time, talent and secretarial skills at my disposal during the editing of the manuscript. Mrs Jackie Kneeshaw corrected and typed the final draft with great wit and humour. Thank you Jackie. A special word of thanks is also owed to Sr Bridget Owens and the Community of Wealdstone, and to Sr Marie Louis who designed the cover. Mike and Joy Byrne whom I met at Barmouth, generously offered to publish the manuscript privately. In the event this was not necessary but it spoke to me of great generosity, kindness and confidence. I also thank Fr Brendan Callaghan for advising me on the manuscript and for agreeing to write the foreword, and Sr Celestine Power who was zealous in providing me with time and space to complete the project. Finally I thank my family for their interest and support in the accomplishment of this work.

I gratefully acknowledge the use of the following materials: Excerpts taken from *The Jerusalem Bible*, published and copyright 1966, 1967 and 1968 by Darton, Longman and Todd Ltd and Doubleday & Co Inc and used by permission of the publishers. Excerpt from *Spiritual Direction and Meditation* by Thomas Merton published by The Liturgical Press and used by permission of the publishers. Excerpt from *The Observer Magazine* by Dr John Collee and used by permission of the publishers. Excerpt from *By Your Touch* (Cassette tape), songs by Jaime Rickert recorded by Parish Mission Team, Suffern NY, permission requested

This book is dedicated in love,
to the memory of my parents, Isabella and John,
who, by word and example, taught me all I know about
Truth, Goodness and Love

Foreword

God's boundless generosity takes as many forms as there are people to receive it, and to allow God to work most fully in us, to allow God's generosity to find full play, each of us needs to allow God to teach us what it is we are being offered – that is, the gifts that God is offering to you, the gifts that God is offering to me, the distinctive ways in which God wishes to enrich your life and my life with sanctity and salvation. Inevitably, each of us also needs to allow God to teach us how we turn away from God's generosity, and how and where to allow God to convert us: the monastic vow of *conversio mori*, conversion of life, reminds us that this is a life-long need. In *Planted in Love* Elizabeth McNulty offers us a way of opening ourselves to this teaching and transforming work of God's Spirit through the medium of the enneagram, as understood in the context of Christian conversion.

Under the guidance of the Holy Spirit, that growth towards sainthood to which we are all called has taken many forms in the history of the Christian community, and many ways have developed of speaking about God's work in us. These different forms of growth and ways of speaking can be seen as embodied in the distinctive charisms of distinctive Christian vocations. The Spirit draws us to the single life, or marriage, or priesthood, or religious community, as men and women who have sensed that in this particular form of life you or I can grow to be the person God longs for us to be. Ways of speaking and understanding have grown up around each of these forms of life, helping to articulate the distinctive work of God in this particular setting. You may find one or other of these speaks to you; I may find that the same or a different one

11

speaks to me. (A great friend who is a monk understands me in all sorts of ways, and often better than I understand myself, but he is as puzzled by the attraction of Ignatian spirituality for me as I am by the attraction of Benedictine spirituality for him.) At the same time, the Christian tradition has been enriched by insights which bridge these different traditions of spirituality, which have something to offer to all Christians, and which can deepen our appreciation of the particular ways in which God has called us.

In our 'psychological age', insights and ways of speaking about God's work in us which relate to our new-found appreciation of human psychology are necessary, and in the enneagram Elizabeth McNulty has found such a way of speaking, and has related it to that constant call to conversion, to a growing openness to God's generosity, which is central to the Christian life. *Planted in Love* is the fruit of much study, but more importantly it is the fruit of much practice. Elizabeth McNulty has spent many years working with men and women who have come to recognise that the enneagram, particularly as it is related to a deep understanding of the nature of conversion, can be a powerful means of opening their lives to God's work.

For those familiar with the enneagram, *Planted in Love* will be an enrichment of their appreciation of what it can offer to men and women who want God to 'convert their lives'. For those who have not come across the enneagram, or who have been uncertain as to whether it has anything to offer to the Christian life, this book will be an introduction to a new way of enabling the work of God's Spirit within us.

'God acts in every person from the interior, the centre of their existence', said Ruysbroeck, centuries before the advent of 'psychology'. I think that he, and many of those who have tried to express something of the wonders of God's transforming work within us, would welcome this contribution to our understanding.

Brendan Callaghan sj
Principal, and lecturer in psychology
Heythrop College, University of London

12

Introduction

In recent years a new psychological 'thriller' has become the topic of conversation in many areas of the English speaking world. I refer to the enneagram. Because of the facility it gives to individuals to observe and examine their own behaviour, the enneagram is recognised as a key to self-knowledge and an effective tool of psychological and spiritual growth. This understanding of human psychology, which comes to us from the Islamic mystical tradition known as Sufism, via South and North America, is both thrilling and profound. It does not teach anything new about human psychology, but brings each one, according to their capacity, to a heightened degree of self-awareness concerning the reality of how things are and of how they personally relate to others. Simple and direct in its presentation the enneagram provides the individual with a profound depth of insight into the mysteries of their own manner of being.

Knowledge of the enneagram in the Western world is still very new. In the 1960's it was being taught by Oscar Ichazo in his school of psychology at Arica in Chile, and from there it was introduced to North America by Claudio Naranjo. In 1974 J.G. Bennett, a disciple of G.I. Gurdjieff, published *The Enneagram* which was later revised and expanded in *Enneagram Studies* published in 1983. Since then numerous other books have been published on the enneagram, however, as a recognised oral tradition of Sufi wisdom it is generally accepted that knowledge of the enneagram is more readily acquired by teaching than reading.

Traditionally, knowledge of the enneagram is passed on orally, and can only be grasped by those who have acquired a degree of self-awareness that ignites a desire for change or personal transformation. For this reason the contents of this book are directed to those who have already acquired the basic teaching of the enneagram in the traditional manner, and who are familiar with its terminology.

The following brief outline of the basic tenets of the enneagram is for the purposes of clarification concerning the subject of the book which is basically about the way in which we resist the grace of spiritual conversion.

The psychological typology presented by the enneagram posits that there are nine basic types of personality, which are designated by the numbers 1-9. These nine types are further sub-divided into three groups of three which are known as the Head, Gut and Heart triads or centres. Thus types # 5, 6 and 7 belong to the Head centre, # 8, 9 and 1 form the Gut centre, and # 2, 3 and 4 are identified as belonging to the Heart centre or triad.

Besides being characterised by particular needs, values and attitudes, each triad of personalities, as defined by the enneagram, is considered to have a marked preference for the use of a particular sense in relating to the environment. Sight is said to be used preferentially by head centred persons, hearing and smelling by those in the gut centre, whilst those in the heart centre favour touch and taste as the manner in which they process reality and relate to and interact with their environment.

Because Christian theology and spirituality recognises that our ability to know, love and serve God and to enter into a loving relationship with him is perceived by the intellect through the medium of the senses the insights of the enneagram concerning the preferential use of the senses suggests there may be a way in which, at the level of personality, we may have a particular interest and focus in relation to the various aspects of conversion.

The great dispensational prophecy of Isaiah which is so frequently quoted in the Gospel seems to me to have a bearing on this

Go and say to this people, 'Hear and hear again
but do not understand,
see and see again, but do not perceive.
Make the heart of this people gross,
its ears are dull,
shut its eyes,
so that it will not see with its eyes,
hear with its ears,
understand with its heart,
and be converted and healed' (Is 6:9).

Consciously hearing this prophecy for the first time was, for me, akin to discovering a 'shadow' side of God by which we are perversely inveigled and trapped into a 'no win' situation of Divine purpose and intent. From a superficial reading of this prophecy it would seem that we are destined by providence to be blind, deaf and hard-hearted in relation to the things of God and our own greater good.

In the Gospel a different tale unfolds, and we see, as it were, the flip-side of the coin, when we witness the frustration of Jesus in dealing with the apostles. Even the privilege of being his chosen companions was no guarantee of their being able to see clearly, hear correctly or respond with understanding. 'O ye of little faith' was a familiar cry of dismay on the lips of Jesus as he variously rebuked their fear (Mt 8:26), their doubt (Mt 14:31), and their lack of understanding (Mt 16:8). The bewilderment of Jesus at the evident lack of faith, hope and reasoning ability of his apostles and disciples clearly exonerates God as the cause of their impaired spiritual seeing, hearing and understanding.

Faith, Hope and Love, seeing, hearing and understanding, these it would appear are radically connected as key elements of Christian conversion in that our ability to believe, hope and love can be limited by our inability to see, hear and understand. Could it be that our impaired seeing, hearing and understanding is of our own making?

15

Like those 'nests' of Russian dolls which open to reveal an identical looking but smaller doll inside, there is one further and final triad of human experience that for me bears relation to conversion. I refer to the three distinct but interconnected aspects of Christian conversion which in his book *Method and Theology*, Bernard Lonergan refers to as intellectual, moral and religious conversion. These, he explains, though related, are each a different aspect of conversion and distinctive type of event, and says that 'intellectual conversion is to truth; moral conversion is to goodness and religious conversion is to love'. Presented in this way I see an evident correlation between intellectual, moral and religious conversion, faith, hope and love and seeing, hearing and understanding.

Applying the typology of the enneagram to the key elements of conversion noted above I wish to suggest ways in which our response to God at the various 'stages' of conversion may be impeded by our unwillingness to move out of our chosen or preferred 'centre of being'. That is to say that by choosing to live within the confines of one triad and by refusing to appreciate the giftedness and possibilities made available to us by the integrated use of all three centres we may be in danger of placing ourselves in the ranks of those who, in the words of the Gospel,

'See and see again
but do not perceive,
hear and hear again,
but do not understand' (Mk 4:12).

This is not to imply or suggest that by the correct and discerning use of all senses we are capable of attaining conversion or holiness by our own efforts or intellectual prowess. I wish simply to recognise that the failure to make adequate use of our senses, intellect, talents and experience may impede the entrance of God into our lives.

Another interesting feature of the enneagram which I wish to consider are the three types of reasoning which it

16

recognises as being characteristic of the three different centres. Logical reasoning is said to be used preferentially by head centred individuals, gut centred individuals are said to reason analogically and heart centred individuals, in general, are considered to use an analytical mode of thinking.

I propose to use the knowledge of the enneagram to explicate how our particular or preferred type of reasoning may also influence our inability or failure 'to see, hear and understand', and is, therefore, important to the whole conversion process.

In presenting the material I have tried to do so in what I consider to be a starkly, simple manner. The reason for this is the desire I have to make clear, lucid connections between the various subjects being dealt with. As an analytical thinker the most difficult task for me has been to work within the framework of a logical, sequential presentation of ideas. I admit to being more at home with a shower of ideas as haphazard and unpredictable as a display of fireworks or a hedgerow of spring flowers.

It is possible that the effort to work within the confines of logical sequence may be reflected in a seemingly dogmatic presentation. I do not wish to imply by this that the process of conversion or intellectual development is predictable. As with any form of growth, the human development and spiritual journey of each individual has a unique pattern, style and rhythm which defies programming, analysis or imitation.

Thinking about thinking

Very often the thing we most dislike about others is their manner of thinking, and the fact that they do not appear to think in the same lucid manner in which we perceive ourselves to reason. The growing awareness that people think or exercise their faculty of reasoning in different ways has, in recent years, caught the attention of educational psychologists with the result that the faculty of reasoning is presently the subject of a number of educational research programmes. Too often in the past emphasis has been placed on what people know rather than how they think in determining reasoning capacity, and frequently, if noticed at all, the importance of their manner of thinking has not been considered. In relation to reasoning, the enneagram recognises logical, analogical and analytical thinking as different and distinct ways of exercising the reasoning faculty of the mind. Furthermore, it suggests that each of these types of reasoning which is subject to different insights and limitations, is extensively and preferentially used by different types of personality.

With the realisation and acceptance that people process experience, information and ideas in a variety of ways, the mechanical process of the 'how' people think is now seen to be just as important as 'what' they think because how we think may have a profound effect on what we think.

In our own country an article in *The Independent* written by Oliver Gillie draws attention to the CASE project conducted by Drs Philip Adey, Michael Sayer and Caroline Yates of Kings College, London. Their findings suggest that there are at least ten basic processes of reasoning which are necessary for effective thinking about the material world, the use of which can facilitate and profoundly effect a person's grasp of a subject. In their research programme they discovered the importance of teaching their students not merely to think, but to 'think how they think'.

To listen to a few discussions or debates on radio or television and observe the different ways in which individuals respond to or process the same facts is convincing evidence that people frequently reason or think differently. If not there would be nothing to discuss. To be attentive to how people think as we listen to such programmes, to pay attention to their line of thought with its particular emphasis and perspective and to notice their distinct pattern of vocabulary and response can often be from the psychological point of view more interesting than the subject being discussed. Even a cursory viewing of such programmes will reveal that people with different personality traits think in a distinctively different manner, irrespective of their levels of intelligence.

That a correlation exists between personality and mode of thinking is, I believe, one of the most beneficial and exciting tenets of the enneagram, and one that to date has not been specifically noted by other schools of psychology. According to the enneagram, the manner in which individuals exercise the faculty of reasoning not only differs from person to person, but is influenced as much by personality as by intellect. That personality has a distinct influence on the manner in which individuals exercise or use the faculty of reasoning, makes it an important factor in determining their learning process and the selection of subjects in which they are likely to excel. This is not to suggest that some personality types are more intelligent than others, but to note that certain personalities are more likely to be gifted in one particular area of intellectual pursuit than in others. In relation to this I believe that different personalities have also a particular affinity with different aspects of conversion. That is to say that cognitive, moral and religious conversion will be given different emphasis or bias according to personality type.

As a corollary of this, knowing how a person thinks

gives the informed and interested observer an insight into that person's personality. This suggests that reasoning and personality influence each other, and that people who have similar personalities will exercise their reasoning faculty in a predictable manner.

An integral tenet of enneagram teaching which is recognised in Christian spirituality and human psychology is that we live only partially and rarely attain our full potential as human beings. In many cases our failure to attain the heights of which we are capable is due to our unwillingness to pay the price required for success in terms of time, dedication, labour and self discipline. In other words, we set limits to our attainments in accordance with the amount of time and energy we are prepared to spend, and so by default condemn ourselves to living below par. If this is true in the development and exercise of talent, may we not suppose it to be equally true in the exercise of our reasoning faculty?

To the extent that we think preferentially in one mode, irrespective of circumstances and in denial of our capacity to think cohesively in all three modes of reasoning as the occasion demands, we may seriously limit the exercise of our reasoning faculty, and ultimately impede our search for truth. That is to say, by limiting ourselves to think in only one mode of reasoning, i.e. logically, analogically or analytically, is to live only partially, because with a little exertion we could avail of all three modes.

In recognising logical, analogical and analytical reasoning as distinct and preferred types of thinking the enneagram would appear to challenge the synonymous use of logic and reasoning in the western world.

If, as the enneagram suggests, we think or process life consistently from a preferred mode of reasoning it may be supposed that our personality will eventually register or respond to the values that are characteristic of that type of reasoning.

For example if logic is my normal mode of reasoning I may find that I have a natural tendency to argue even about

MODES OF REASONING

According to the enneagram each triad of personalities is said to have a preference for a particular mode of reasoning.

HEAD centred personalities are said to reason logically, GUT personalities are said to reason analogically, and HEART centred people to reason analytically.

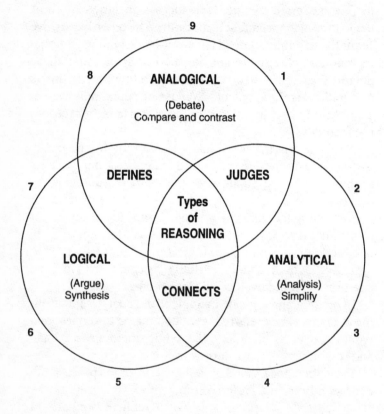

The integrated use of all three modes of reasoning enables us to define clearly, judge correctly and identify concisely, whatever we desire or need to know about a subject.

inconsequential matters, or have a fear of accepting any new thinking. This could impede an ongoing search for truth.

If I consistently think analogically, I should not be surprised to find myself contesting the cherished opinions of others, or evaluating their actions with a critical and dismissive mind. Analytical thinkers suffer from a compulsion to analyse everything and everyone often without any thought of the sensitivity of their remarks and of the great discomfort these may cause to those present.

Though logic, analogic and analysis are integral units of the faculty of reasoning the three processes are frequently used independently as though complete and even at times in opposition to each other. This partial and divisive manner of thinking can be detrimental to an integrated process of reasoning.

Reasoning and conversion

As has already been noted in the introduction conversion involves three interrelated, yet distinguishable components, i.e. intellectual, moral and religious conversion. That each of these elements are parts of the whole process does not change the fact that each part requires distinctly different responses, processes and graces.

As defined by Bernard Lonergan cognitive conversion is the process of coming to a knowledge of truth as revealed by God. Moral conversion is the process of choosing goodness as the means of living in a Christ like way. And finally, affective conversion is the process of coming to an understanding and appreciation of the relationships which bind and unite us in love with God and each other. In inviting us to conversion, God respects our intelligence and free will and never forces our acceptance.

Because reasoning plays an integral role in what we believe, in the selection of factors that influence our decisions and in our understanding of relationships, it must also play an integral role within each element of conversion and thereby may affect conversion as a whole. This is not to deny that the process of conversion requires more than intellectual or reasoning ability, a fact that is evidenced by the number of intellectual atheists and agnostics. Lonergan says that religious conversion actually 'dismantles and abolishes' the horizon of our knowing and choosing, thus setting us on a new plane on which God 'transvalues and transforms our knowing' (Method p. 106).

Likewise, Paul Robb in *Conversion as a Human Experience* states that the kind of self knowledge required for affective conversion is not analytical knowledge. He describes affective self knowledge as an intimate understanding of self which can only be learned about through relationships, the experience of life and the grace of conversion (*Human* p. 24).

In *Spiritual Direction and Meditation*, Thomas Merton addresses the relationship of reasoning to meditation. He writes:

'Strictly speaking, even religious meditation is primarily a matter of thought. But it does not end in thought. Meditation is not merely a matter of "thinking things out" even if it leads to good ethical resolution' (pp. 45-46).

Merton then defines the 'distinctive characteristic' of religious meditation as a search for truth which springs from love. By recognising that thought is a fundamental requirement in relation to religious meditation, Merton opens the door to reasoning as a requirement in relation to conversion.

In his Spiritual Exercises, Saint Ignatius states that 'fallacious reasonings' are used by the evil one to keep us from that true happiness which is the gift of God (*Exercises* p. 147). Thus according to Saint Ignatius, reasoning is an integral part of our relationship with God. There seems no doubt that the gift of reasoning can assist or hinder us in our search for God.

What each of the above authors suggests is that in relation to conversion and Divine truth human reason is inadequate. Earlier we saw how Christ was dismayed at the fallacious reasonings of his apostles. This suggests to me that the manner in which we think can effect either negatively or positively our response to truth, goodness and love, which are the subject of conversion.

Principle and foundation
of conversion

On one occasion, as a member of the panel of BBC's *Question Time* Terry Waite was asked to name in three words the qualities he would most like to characterise the next Prime Minister. 'Intelligence, Compassion and Integrity', was his terse reply. The quickness and sincerity with which he made his choice provoked in me a happy smile as I mused on the possibility that one day these desirable attributes might universally be recognised as essential traits of all those seeking election to parliament. Just imagine the transformation that would be possible for a society blessed with such enlightened leadership.

Following this pipe dream a more serious reflection led me to consider that if we understand 'intelligence' to mean an ongoing 'search for truth', it is not difficult to correlate the characteristics listed by Terry Waite with the great triad of theological virtues, Faith, Hope and Charity which are the principle and foundation of the Christian religion. I say this, because in Christian spirituality, Faith, which opens our minds and hearts to God, makes us adhere to God by engaging our intellect and senses in the pursuit of knowledge and truth; Hope is rooted in compassion – the saving compassion of God; and Integrity is the flower and fruit of Charity. These three virtues which we receive at Baptism, are recognised by Christian theology as the essential Christian human response to the Divine revelation that we are created, saved and loved by God.

Called theological virtues because they pertain directly to God, Faith, Hope and Charity have God as their source and immediate object. The gift of these virtues, which is infused at Baptism, enables us to participate in God's own life and animates us to witness and respond to the God whom by revelation we 'know and understand' to be faithful, compassionate and loving. In other words, God, who is faithful, is the source and object of our faith, the God of compassion is the source of our kindness, hope and joy, and God who is Charity is the primary end, motive and author of our love.

Since God who is infinite is at once the object and goal, the source and inspiration of our response, the human limitations of our practise of faith, hope and charity will never be totally adequate to the gift we have received. Always there will be something more to know and understand about God, and always some other direction in which to extend and enhance our response. By deepening our knowledge of God, growth in the practise of these virtues also deepens our awareness and appreciation of ourselves and others as people created, saved and loved by God.

Because in essence, each contains the other two, Faith, Hope and Charity are not so much three separate virtues as three distinct facets of the same charism or gift. By the grace and gift of the theological virtues our senses are alerted to the activity of God in the world, our faculties are adapted for participation in the Divine Life and our lives are radiated by the warmth of Divine Love.

It is important to note that even though made inoperative by sin, Faith and Hope can subsist without Charity, since it is possible to believe in God without loving Him and to hope in God whilst in a state of sin or separation from God. Charity cannot, however, subsist without Faith and Hope, nor co-exist with sin which is the denial or betrayal of Love. It is this absolute character of Charity which makes it indispensable to our spiritual lives, and crowns it as the queen of virtues:

'In short, there are three things that last:
Faith, Hope and Love;
and the greatest of these is Love' (1 Co 13:13).

27

ASPECTS OF CONVERSION

Religious conversion is a process of spiritual maturation and self-transcendence, initiated by God.

It involves the individual in an on-going search for *truth, goodness* and *love*, which according to Bernard Lonergan are the goals of *cognitive*, *moral* and *religious conversion*, respectively.

In accordance with their preferential mode of reasoning I believe that each triad of personalities has a particular preference for one aspect of conversion. HEAD personalities appear to focus on truth, GUT personalities are attracted to goodness and HEART personalities are dominated by love.

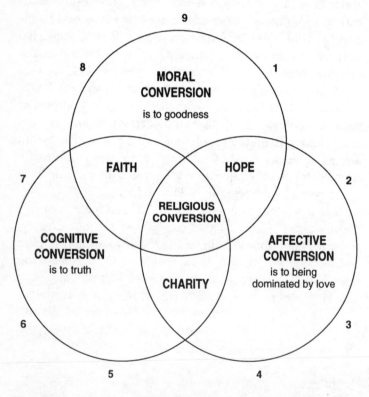

The desire for *truth*, *goodness* and *love*, is activated in us by the theological virtues of *faith, hope* and *charity*.

It is by Divine Revelation that God sets in motion that dynamic process of personal transformation we refer to as conversion. The fullness of revelation has been given to us in the person of Christ, whom we call Emmanuel or 'God with us'. Philip de Rosato says that in his human nature 'Christ shows us the Divine way of being Human'. In Christ we discover all that can be known of God here on earth, for in his own person Christ shows forth the fidelity, compassion and love of our God, and exemplifies for us the most perfect human response to God, of a life that is lived in truth with compassion and love.

Having said that conversion, which is initiated by God, is characterised by the practise of Faith, Hope and Charity, I wish to look at the transformation these particular virtues effect in the lives of those who make them their rule of life. Initially, however, I propose to look at the distinctive characteristics of each triad of personalities as defined by the enneagram.

Characteristics of the three centres

Ever since Saint Augustine prayed 'Let me know myself, Lord, and I shall know you,' it has been recognised in Christian spirituality that self-knowledge is the essential foundation for any true encounter with God. To this end, all the sciences which promote self-knowledge and self-understanding are considered to be elementary tools of spiritual growth. The enneagram, which is a descriptive system of personality types is one such tool.

A basic tenet of enneagram teaching is that early in life each person makes a fundamental decision, in relation to self-protection, which becomes a determining factor of their personality. This decision, which is made unconsciously, leads each of us to shut off or devalue a vital area of human experience. In other words we go through life with the determination to avoid or block what is in fact an essential and unavoidable experience of human life and growth. The avoidance, which is compulsive by nature, effectively becomes a protective mask or 'persona' preventing knowledge of the true self. Discovery of our own particular mask, persona or number, is merely the first step in coming to an appreciation and acceptance of the whole self.

Another fundamental teaching of the enneagram is that our personality is 'the psyche manifestation of one of the major physiological systems of the body' (Oscar Ichazo). This gives rise to the theory that each person lives distinctly and by preference from one particular area of the body. That is to say there are what are commonly named head, heart and gut personalities, each with their distinctive traits of character.

These three systems of physiological activity are considered by the enneagram to identify three basic instincts of survival and growth. The instinct of syntony or of being in tune is said to be related to the nervous system, the focal point of which is in the head. The conservation instinct is located in the gut which is the centre of the digestive and alimentary system, and the relational instinct is heart based in the organ which controls the circulatory system.

Another distinguishing characteristic of each centre or triad of personalities is the manner in which energy is used. Water in its three forms of gas, liquid and ice, is used by Oscar Ichazo as a metaphor for the different and distinct types of energy used by head, heart and gut types.

Therefore, in relation to the enneagram the use of energy is one of the most obvious ways of discovering one's triad or centre. This does, however, presuppose a certain facility for self-observation, which a surprisingly high number of individuals appear to lack. The simple question 'Where was your energy at that moment?' can often draw a blank from those who are not accustomed to observing their own behaviour and use of energy.

Because we each have a head, a heart and a gut all three types of psychological and physical growth and survival are available to us and when used in unison they provide us with a richly balanced and integrated facility for survival, growth and maturation. However, according to the enneagram, even in intelligent and mature individuals one centre frequently predominates to the detriment of the other two and as a consequence of this unbalanced use of our faculties our capacity for survival, growth and healthy development is seriously impeded or diminished.

A final clue that may help us to discover the triad from which we operate is that of speech. Our perception of life and the values we promote are often revealed in our manner of speaking. Head personalities who seek enlightenment frequently use language associated with light, gut people in my experience exercise a preference for language that is related to hearing and balance and heart centred people refer to feelings.

31

In his delineation of the three basic instincts, Oscar Ichazo ascribes particular characteristics to each of the centres or systems. The following simplified but detailed overview of these characteristics is offered as an outline sketch for purposes of clarification. It is not my intention to imply that the values and options of a preferred or predominant centre are always lived in a radical manner by individual persons. The normal process of maturation will ensure that there will be a greater or lesser level of integration of the centres in each individual, according to personal circumstances.

Characteristics of the head centre (5, 6, 7)

Physical location: head and nervous system

Head centred personalities are said to approach life from the head which encases the brain and controls the nervous system of the body, and both these faculties are said to play a significant part in the personality development and profile of these individuals.

Because the brain controls the processes of learning and memory, the head is regarded as the centre of thought and intellectual power. The location of the brain within the skull, plus the fact that, of itself, the brain has no feeling, is given as the reason why head personalities are able to function mainly from the intellectual perspective with little or no regard for feelings.

The brain is also the organ which controls the process of sensation, and the lack of 'feeling' that is characteristic of head personalities may in some way be assuaged or replaced by a capacity for empathy which is related to comprehension.

The nervous system, which is also centred in the head, is the means by which the body co-ordinates its activity in relation to its environment. To be 'in tune' with their surroundings and environment and to fit in with expectations of those in authority are characteristic traits of those who operate by preference from this centre. Their need to conform and accommodate their actions to the wishes or directives of others can create a certain dependency on others and nervous tension may occur should they find themselves at variance with the group.

Senses used preferentially

In order to relate to their environment head people need to see, and this preferential use of sight as their contact with reality makes them more likely than others to be in touch with events and situations which are at a distance rather than with those which are imminent. Figuratively speaking, they can see the fly on the wall but not the nose on their face. In a very real sense 'out of sight' is 'out of mind' for those who function from this centre.

Because of the emphasis given to sight by this group they possess a facility for projecting and planning, and a sagacity in discerning future requirements, which make them an asset to any planning committee. An added dimension of their foresight and capacity for long distance viewing is that they tend to live in the future and are often more at ease with future and past events than with those of the present.

Basic instinct – vital concern

It has long been recognised that the most basic human instinct is that of survival. Each of us is born with an innate impulse and unconscious skill to survive and grow. The enneagram proposes that in response to this instinct the principle of 'syntony' or of 'being in tune' becomes the chosen means of survival and growth of head personalities. Being in harmony with creation and society, as mentioned above is, therefore, of vital concern for head personalities as this provides them with a secure basis of survival and growth.

In their perception harmony arising from a consistent, agreeable and orderly manner of life facilitates the establishment of a stable and just society. Every stage and aspect of life, every event or eventuality is observed by head personalities, to be governed and controlled by natural, physical or civic law which, when acknowledged and adhered to, bring individuals and society into harmony with the universe.

Conformity to these laws is considered to be a basic ingredient of a secure and happy life, and any deliberate deviation from them a possible cause of chaos, destruction and perhaps even annihilation. The observance of law and allegiance to authority which may be perceived to be the embodiment of truth and the fountain of knowledge, may be demanded by head personalities as a test of loyalty to the group.

The advantage of such reasoning is obvious. In an ordered, well regulated family, community or society, everyone and everything has an appropriate and designated position, rank and function. Each one knows their place and role; they know where they are and what is expected of them; they know what to do and how to act. The vital questions addressed to life by the head centred personalities 'Where am I?'; 'What do I do in this situation?'; are thus answered. Authority and law provide each of them with a framework in which to function with security, whilst at the same time contributing to the well being of society as a whole. As long as order is maintained everyone benefits. However, any deviant behaviour on the part of an individual or group within the community, any challenge to authority is perceived to be dangerous to all. As Dr Seuss so aptly explains, if 'Yertle the Turtle' refuses to be a loyal member of the team supporting the 'throne', then we may all end up in the mud, and chaos will ensue.

Values

The above perception of truth or reality will, of necessity, give high priority to law enforcement, respect for legitimate authority, and the responsibility of the individual in respect to society. Loyalty, obedience, conformity and docility are seen to be admirable qualities, and to be in accord and empathy with others the essential human requirements for the establishment of a benevolent and stable society.

Harmony is such a desirable state for head centred personalities that it may blind them to other more important issues and when this happens they may settle for a state of imposed regimentation which is a denial of the most basic principles of harmony.

Domination

Head centred personalities are said to be dominated by authority. The need to have authority, and also to be 'an authority' gives drive and colour to their personalities. According to their perception right vested in authority is the binding force and guiding light which gives cohesion, direction and purpose to the group. Assenting to the directions and teachings of those in authority creates an ambience of peace and security. In their desire to conform and fit in, to be in unity with the group, head people will rarely challenge authority. To do so would be self-destructive.

This respect for, and dependence on, authority is evident in all areas of life, and may be observed in the respect they have for creeds, dogmas, rituals and traditions, as well as in their dependency on dictionaries, maps, directions and regulations. All are authoritative guides which promote unity and conformity by providing the drum beat to which all may march in unison. The observance of tradition and custom in time honoured rituals are ways of ensuring that the values of the past are handed on to the next generation. Such helps are also a door to knowledge and a guard against ignorance.

Problems

Head centred people have problems with insecurity and fear. Relying as they do on authority, they carry a sense of responsibility to conform to what others may decide is in the interest of the common good. 'Rules are rules' can be a compelling motivation for acting contrary to their own convictions, loyalty can be a burden, but deviance is too fearful to contemplate. Their fear may be expressed in their ability to 'turn a blind eye' to an authority which is corrupt and unjust. It is possible that they may confuse legality with morality, and feel justified in accepting questionable practises from others which they would not allow or tolerate in themselves.

Another problem they have is the desire to be always 'right'. They have a great regard for truth and in general are well informed, but should they be confronted by evidence which is new to them their insecurity or lack of trust may cause them to 'quibble' before grudgingly conceding a point. They may be less than generous with those who make a discovery, or arrive at a truth before they do.

Reasoning

Reasoning in the head centre is logical, clear, lucid and defined. Since the purpose of logic is to clinch an argument logical thinkers deal with evidence and proof in an ordered and methodical way. There is no place for the imagination in this type of thinking, which is of necessity factual, literal and systematic.

Energy

The energy of head centred individuals has been compared to gas, vapour or mist, which can be powerful and hidden, explosive and intense. Such energy can reach for the sky, or fizzle out as a damp squid.

Frequently the energy of head centred individuals is devoted to planning to such an extent that what is future is given a disproportionate amount of their energy, leaving their resources depleted for present use. They can weary themselves with worrying about the probable or the possible and leave little or no reserves for the actual.

Speech

Perhaps it is the importance of the 'visual' to their learning process, that causes head centre personalities to rely heavily on the language of sight when expressing themselves. For example, they talk about 'insight', ask for 'clarification' or make plans in the 'light' of what has been discussed. 'Show me', 'I see', 'I'm not blind', 'I think...' may be expressions they frequently use.

It is important for head centred personalities to see evidence in order to be convinced, 'unless I see... I will not believe'. They are said to be more easily accepting of the written word than of hearsay, but may be 'blinded' by facts even when presented in writing, and in argument or debate may attempt to 'dazzle' others with their knowledgeable presentation of facts and statistics.

Characteristics of the gut centre (8, 9, 1)

Physical location: gut and alimentary and digestive system

The gut, bowels or entrails are the physical location from which gut centred personalities are said to operate, and, being the area of the body where life is generated, conceived and nurtured, this centre is regarded as the centre of

37

life and living. To say that someone has 'guts' is to imply that they have character, courage, pluck and forceful energy.

Because the pelvic region, which contains the gut, is the body's centre of gravity, this centre is also recognised as the centre of balance, movement and co-ordination. Precision, poise and equilibrium, which are essential components of balance are characteristic of this centre and facilitate the physical gift of dance and movement, and the rational gifts of judgement and discernment with which gut people are blessed.

The functioning of the alimentary and digestive system is also influential in determining the personality profile of people who live preferentially from this centre. The processes of assimilation, digestion and purgation which have to do with the maintenance of healthy living and bodily cleansing are of interest and concern to them, and this interest is not confined to merely physical cleansing but is reflected in their abhorrence or rejection of whatever they judge to be intellectual, political or moral corruption. In their desire for cleansing and 'purity' they tend to favour radical solutions to problems and may advocate a 'fresh start' or a 'clean sweep' as the only way forward.

Gut centred personalities are said to function with instincts and habits and often without thinking, so this centre is known as the instinctive centre. As people of habit, their knowing how to act arises from an instinctive reaction that is rooted in practise and past experience.

Senses used preferentially

Hearing and smelling, which are considered to be the most primitive of the senses and the first line of defence against life threatening situations are used preferentially by gut centre personalities in their interaction with their environment.

The preferential use of these senses is often evident in the facility that gut personalities have for music, language, movement, dance and sport. As an organ of balance the ear performs a duel function or purpose, in relation to these gifts.

Their sensitivity to smell makes fresh air, pure water and open spaces essential ingredients of life so they will normally enjoy outdoor activities, and may surround themselves with plants, even indoors. Although they have a capacity for life and living which is robust, energetic and vital, their preoccupation with healthy living may cause them to become hypochondriacs. They probably keep the health food stores in business.

Basic instinct – vital concern

Vital concern relates to our perception of what constitutes reality. The vital concern for gut centred people is 'being' or existence because what is real or true for them is the fact of being alive, of being well and healthy. The maintenance, conservation and preservation of life, which is their basic concern, is not just about survival and existence, but about the quality and essence of life, and the ability to acquire the power and energy which quickens and sustains life.

'How am I?' which is the basic question they address to life, exposes their concern and preoccupation with their physical, spiritual, social and emotional well-being. It is a question which immediately introduces the need to compare and contrast, to make a judgement, 'Am I good or better?'; 'Am I healthy or sick?'; 'Am I right or wrong?'; 'Is this fair or just?'. Their gut reactions to these questions is generally the one that is most appropriate and correct, and the one that will dictate the path of survival.

At the gut level, reality is measured by the quality or essence of life it engenders, and authenticity is, for them, the essence of truth.

The particular bias of gut personalities in their perception of reality will focus on the essential requirements of life, and the avoidance of death. For gut personalities a person's right to life and freedom is paramount, and presupposes access to the means of pursuing life, liberty, peace and happiness, irrespective of class, culture or race. Therefore, equality, justice, freedom and human rights have priority values for people who operate preferentially from this centre.

In their desire for life, gut centred personalities are prepared to assume the role of challenging any abuse of human rights or any infringement of liberty, no matter who the perpetrators may be. They are the prophets who denounce the abuses of society which harm or destroy the freedom, reputation and life of the individual, and the crusaders who champion the rights of the weak and marginalised, and who work to destroy evil. Their need to defend 'life' and annihilate 'evil' can be very problematic for gut personalities especially if someone has the audacity to question: 'whose life, whose evil?'

More than a legitimate right, confrontation is considered to be a social obligation and their prophetical and confrontational stance may make gut personalities the goad of tyrants, or the bane of hedonists. They seem to live by the principle that as the divinely appointed custodians of creation we promote life by protecting our inheritance which is also our responsibility.

Domination

Gut centred people are dominated by power or energy. They need to possess it, they need to control it. Power gives energy, life and freedom, whoever has power can survive, those without power will die. As human beings we all have a right to power, a right to life, a right to freedom. To empower people is to quicken and sustain life, and to disempower them is to weaken and destroy life. Power, therefore, as the key to life is to be guarded jealously. 'Who has the power?'; 'Who controls the source of energy?'; 'How is it being used?'; these are questions of vital concern to gut centred personalities. The answer given to their questions will decide their course of action.

Because of their preoccupation with power, gut centred personalities have a compulsion to avoid what they consider to be weakness and are reluctant to relinquish control of their lives to anyone, as for example in allowing others to take control of the car in which they are travelling. They like to be in the driving seat.

Problems

Gut centred personalities have problems with indecision and repression of their feelings. The enneagram clearly teaches what is a recognised fact of psychology, namely that our strengths are also our weaknesses. In this centre, which by reason of its balanced approach to life good judgement is a gift, people often have difficulty in making decisions. Their desire to sift all available information, to compare and contrast, to weigh up all the variables, to be meticulously precise, fair and exact will, at times, make it well nigh impossible for them to come to a reasoned decision.

The main problem seems to be that of refusing to accept that they have sufficient information on which to make a 'correct and balanced' judgement. They are sticklers for 'perfection' just as head personalities are sticklers for 'rules'.

Another reason for their dilatory approach to decision making is their need to be 'free'. Decision presumes commitment, and gut personalities like to hedge their bets or leave their options open, which means that they frequently 'dither' when confronted by the need to decide.

This is evident not only in critical life and death situations, but in the trivia of every day living. Having decided they need a new pair of shoes it may take them several months to actually purchase them, and I suspect that those members of the party who find it difficult to make a choice from the menu without consulting the waiter are gut personalities.

Human biology teaches that the gut is the most exposed and vulnerable of all our organs because it lacks a protective bone structure. In psychological terms this may explain why Gut personalities have problems with their feelings. They are very sensitive and vulnerable as regards feelings and will try to deny or repress them because they are considered to be signs of weakness. They have the capacity to blot out unpleasant or challenging experiences by 'turning a deaf ear', and will take flight from what they perceive to be dangerous or unpleasant situations.

Reasoning

According to the enneagram, reasoning in the gut centre is analogical, precise, measured and balanced. The purpose of analogical reasoning is to evaluate, weigh, measure and consider all available information in order to make informed and viable choices.

The need of gut personalities to constantly judge and evaluate situations may give to others who do not belong to this centre a feeling of being continually assessed or criticised by the analogical thinker. This can have an intimidating effect on others.

In an article in the *The Sunday Times Magazine*, Dr John Collee writes of the gut having a mind of its own:

'Our conventional view of how the body is organised has the brain and the spinal cord at the top of an administrative hierarchy with all the other organs blindly obeying instructions. It has become increasingly apparent, however, that quite a lot of organs are capable of thinking for themselves. The heart will pump in a co-ordinated way even when disconnected from its nerve supply and that humble organ the gut, has a mind all of its own.'

Whilst the enneagram does not impute reasoning to the physical organs after which the centres are named, it does suggest that each centre has its own particular brand of reasoning.

Energy

The energy of gut personalities is said to be like ice – solid, transparent, brittle and colourless. Depending on circumstances their energy can be slow moving or rapid, intense or powerful, indolent or vigorous. As with ice, the energy of gut centred personalities can be loud and immediate.

The explosive burst of energy followed by periods of prolonged rest which is characteristic of those who operate from the gut centre, seem to pattern the slow digestive and rapid expurgative process of the alimentary tract. In imitation of the digestive system after which the centre is named, their energy appears to have a natural rhythmic flow of prolonged assimilation and explosive purgation.

Speech

Gut people frequently act instinctively which leaves them open to the accusation of thinking only after they have acted. Their ability to act in this way stems from their preference of 'living in the past', and it is the accumulation of past experiences which gives them the confidence of 'knowing' how to act now. They frequently use words or expressions that are associated with knowing and hearing, such as 'I know'; 'Tell me... ' 'Do you hear me?' They also pass judgement on others without appearing to be aware of it, as for example when overtaken by another driver, 'He must be doing 80'.

They may find it necessary to 'digest' information, and may reply in a hesitant or thoughtful manner as they search for the exact nuance to convey their meaning. In striking contrast they may also blast their 'opponent' with strong and abusive language as they struggle to find the most offensive and aggressive expletive to express their frustration.

Characteristics of the heart centre (2, 3, 4)

Physical location: heart and circulatory system

The heart, which controls the circulatory system, is the physical location from which heart centred personalities are said to operate. In Christian theology this is recognised as the centre of spirituality, and is universally recognised as the centre of love, intimacy, friendship and emotions. It is also recognised by the enneagram as the centre of intuition.

The activity of the heart in circulating nourishment, blood and oxygen to the entire body means that it is in constant touch with every other organ and physical function of the body and the primary source of their health and well-being. The heart is therefore recognised as the body's centre of communication, and is the natural bridge between the other two centres because of the central location it occupies in the body.

The blood which flows through our veins and is kept in circulation by the heart carries the key to our parentage and establishes our unique identity. We talk about being related by 'blood' and say of close friends that they are 'kindred' spirits or even 'blood brothers'. The heart is therefore the centre of relationships.

As with the other two centres each of the above factors

is influential in determining the personality profile of those who live preferentially from this centre.

Senses used preferentially

In relating to their environment heart people make preferential use of the senses of touch and taste. They are 'tactile' persons, for whom touch and taste are important experiences and have a need to 'feel' and 'savour' an experience in order to understand it. By producing an effect of solidarity, touch helps them to express concern, influence, effect or impress, all of which are important elements of their desire to be in relationship.

Generally speaking they are 'in touch' with trends and styles, and have a flair for fashion and a keen sense of colour. Often they are good cooks, and will rely on taste, experience and talent rather than cookery books when preparing a meal.

Basic instinct – vital concern

Being in relationship is of vital concern to heart centred personalities, who cannot 'survive' without friends. Life, or reality for them is to be in touch, to be in communication, to be in relationship. According to their understanding, love alone can reveal to us the mystery of being and the purpose of life. For heart centred personalities love is what life and reality are all about. In the absence of love, in the absence of relationships life is untenable.

'Who am I?' is the basic question they address to life. Because identity is discovered and defined in terms of relationships, this question can only be answered by recognising and acknowledging the relationships that bind us to others.

Like our fingerprints or genetic code, the network of relationships into which a person is born is unique to each individual. To the extent that relationships survive death, for example in family trees, they are even more specialised than fingerprints in defining who I am. Therefore, to know and recognise my family and kinsfolk is essential in the quest for self-knowledge and personal identity.

As they key to identity, relationships reveal to us the truth about ourselves and others, and are therefore at the heart of our instinct for survival.

Values

As with the other two centres, the values of heart centred people are related to their understanding of truth and what life is about. Relationships are their yard-stick. If my relationships are good then I must be good. If my relationships are inadequate, then I, too, am inadequate.

Given this perspective and priority it is easy to comprehend the heart centred person's need to forge wholesome, healthy, impressive and advantageous relationships.

The qualities and characteristics valued by heart centred individuals are considered to be related to their need to discover their true selves, impress others and make friends. Accomplishment, position, education, image and social background are important values as these are considered to be the factors which will promote successful and happy relationships. Names are also significant, as they recognise the unique identity of the individual; and titles also, as these create an aura of nobility and grandeur.

The manner in which heart personalities are addressed or spoken to is critical to their own self-appreciation as it reveals the respect or lack of respect in which they are held by others. Honesty and integrity, which are the principle and foundation of any sincere and wholesome friendship are characteristic of this centre.

Domination

Heart centred people are dominated by image. The importance to them of relationships and consequent need of friendship makes it essential for them to be recognised as someone worth knowing. This need for recognition and the desire to 'belong' has the effect of making them very preoccupied with their image, as they strive to make themselves attractive and acceptable to others. How they appear to others, what others think of them becomes central to their own self-awareness and self-evaluation. Unfortunately, their need to project a good image in order to acquire friends may leave them open to duplicity and deceit. Whilst sincerely striving for honesty and integrity, they are not adverse to gilding the 'lily' should they perceive it to be tarnished.

If failure threatens to engulf heart centred personalities they may 'package' the unpalatable facts about family, friends, or business in an attempt to avoid censure or painful exposure. In turn they may be easily hoodwinked by the impressive but false image projected by others and be dazzled by baubles. Paradoxically, in their desire to create an impressive image, heart personalities may distance themselves and stand aloof from those who, given the opportunity, would appreciate and value their friendship.

People in this centre have a compulsion to avoid failure as this would be seen to reflect adversely on their image. They are also attention seekers.

Problems

Persons who operate from the heart centre have problems with independence and anxiety. In spite of their need for acceptance and friendship, heart personalities are often cold and distant for though they desire to have close friendships they are protective of their privacy and independence, and may shun the exposure that intimacy implies. Above and beyond all friendship or liaison heart centred people

47

have a need to be 'me', and to discover their own identity.

People in this centre have problems with personal boundaries, and appear to be attracted and repulsed by friendship at one and the same time. This would appear to come from the conflict or dilemma that exists for them in wanting to be loved and understood whilst fearing to be known. There is always the possibility that 'if people know me they may not like me' and this is a cause of great anxiety to them.

The propensity they have for friendship, added to their fear of it, exposes them to the accusation of being flirtatious or insincere and they may appear to others to 'dabble' in relationships, in what is generally referred to as having a 'rag on every bush'. Their apparent lack of commitment to a group may stem from a sense of not belonging or of not being identified with the group.

Reasoning

Reasoning in the heart centre is analytical. The purpose of analytical reasoning is to understand and establish the nature and function of relationships and inter-relatedness. This understanding which is acquired by a process of identification, relationship, connectedness and analysis, and is circuitous in process, aims to discover and identify the underlying principle of unity governing all relationships.

Energy

The energy in the heart centre is said to be like water, which never ceases flowing day nor night. Unlike the brain and the gut, the heart cannot stop its vital activity. What it can do is to change rhythm, to move slowly, even languidly, or rapidly and erratically.

Heart people like to be occupied, and despite what others may say, are capable of doing more than one thing at a time, as for example when they iron clothes and keep their attention on the meal they are preparing. Heart people tend to live in the here and now and are concerned with their own and others' needs at the present moment.

Speech

Individual who operate preferentially from the heart centre will tell you how they 'feel' about things, rather than what they think. As they constantly look for understanding they will be at pains to be understood and will enquire 'do you understand, do you get my meaning?' In conversation their line of thought appears to imitate the action of the heart as they talk in a roundabout way and seem compelled to touch on each and every connected detail. Others may find it impossible to follow this apparently disconnected flow of speech.

Another characteristic of heart speech is that of referring to people as 'what's-his-name' and to articles as 'what-d'you-call-it' or the 'thingummyjig'. This 'perverse' and annoying habit is almost sufficient to drive precise gut personalities to a state of temporary insanity! It is a temptation that heart people must learn to resist.

At times heart people can be pensively silent and appear withdrawn from the group. This is also a form of communication.

The diagram overleaf gives a summary of the distinctive characteristics of each triad or centre as defined by the enneagram.

From the above it is evident that each triad of personalities exercises distinct and definitive options in relation to their physical, intellectual, emotional and social development. That these preferential norms should be influential in determining their perception and appreciation of the various aspects of conversion seems fairly obvious.

In the following chapters I propose to consider some of these influences in respect to Faith, Hope and Charity.

SUMMARY TABLE OF 3 TRIADS

Centre	Head 5, 6, 7	Gut 8, 9, 1	Heart 2, 3, 4,
Physical Location	Head and nervous system	Alimentary tract and digestive system	Heart and circulatory system
Preferential use of senses	Sight	Hearing and smelling	Touch and taste
Space	Future	Past	Present
Vital Concern	To be in tune (syntony)	To be alive (conservation)	To be in relationship (belonging)
Vital question	Where am I?	How am I?	Who am I?
Values	Harmony law and order security, conformity	Homeostasis equilibrium, fair play, justice, peace and freedom	Identity family, relationships, character, education
Domination	Authority – law	Power – control	Image – identity
Problems	Insecurity and fear	Indecision and repression	Independence and anxiety
Reasoning	Logical	Analogical	Analytical
Energy	Vapour misty, steam cloudy, distant	Solid immediate instinctual	Liquid flowing, channelled, invasive
Speech	I think	I know	I feel

Faith

A few years ago a friend sent me a picture postcard which depicted two little birds in the branches of a tree growing by the side of a busy thoroughfare. At a great distance below them the scene was one of feverish activity, of 'Lowery like' people hastening about their affairs with anxious and concentrated concern. The caption read 'What a pity they do not know they have a heavenly father'. That, in essence, is what faith is about, it is the conviction and comfort of knowing that we have a heavenly father who loves and cares for us.

The symbol used to depict religious faith is light, the Divine light of God which dispels the darkness of ignorance and doubt and illuminates our mind in relation to Divine truth. By putting us in contact with the transcendent, imminent and eternal reality of God who is our one and only truth, faith illuminates our intellect and gives us clarity of vision concerning the essential reality of the meaning and purpose of life, which is to know, love and praise God.

In the absence of faith we are in darkness and have no means of coming to a knowledge of God, but the gift of faith ignites in us a belief in God which illuminates for us the evidence of God's presence in the world, in creation and in the daily events of life. We believe in God only in virtue of God having made himself known to us. Faith is, therefore, the foundation and principle of our relationship with God, and the means by which we respond to the evidence of God's presence in our lives. This theological gift is not something that can be grasped by the intellect alone because in giving us access to the life of God Faith takes us beyond the boundaries of human reason and of sense perception. Even though at the level of natural intelligence it is possible to discover evidence of a hidden God or supreme force sustaining and directing the universe, it is not intellect but revelation that puts us in contact and relationship with that same God. Human intelligence may inform us regarding the intricate natural laws that sustain the universe but only faith can put us in contact with the author of those same laws. Just as we need a microscope to discover the intricate and unique pattern of every snowflake, and a telescope to view the rings of Saturn, more so do we require the gift of faith to discover the evidence of God's presence in the universe. Transcending all natural powers of reasoning, faith is the means given to us by God which makes us privy to the mystery of God's inner, triune life.

Another important characteristic of light that pertains to faith is that it dispels coldness and radiates warmth and comfort. Besides illuminating the mind, faith is the light which infuses the life of the believer with warmth and comfort by generating in us a trust and confidence which is rooted in the assurance of God's faithful love and providential care.

To have faith in God is to trust him implicitly. It is to know, with an inner conviction, that we have a heavenly Father who has our best interest at heart. People of strong faith are often characterised by the confidence and trust with which they relate to God, and even – dare we say it- by their spirit of abandonment to Divine providence (cf Mt 6:25-34). This, in truth, is the measure of our faith, that we trust in God in all the vicissitudes of life, knowing that his love will always 'arise before the dawn' and will carry us through the day. Frequently, those who are inspired by faith with a desire to know God more intimately, are invited to '... leave everything'. The Divine invitation to leave all for the kingdom of God and to abandon ourselves to Divine providence is, I believe, the gift of 'evangelical poverty'. A life cluttered with material possessions can seriously impede our reliance on God as the source of our well-being and happiness. To be tethered by 'consumerism' or an inordinate love of material goods may prevent our seeking first and foremost 'the kingdom of God'. In the Gospel parable of the rich young man we have evidence that God invites this level of trust (cf Mt 19:21).

Twice in the Gospel is it recorded that Jesus was amazed, and on both occasions it was in relation to the exercise and practice of faith. On the first occasion he was astonished by the faith of the pagan centurion (cf Mt 8:10), and on the second occasion by the lack of faith of his disciples (cf Mt 6:6). It was because of the confident faith of his followers that Jesus was able to work miracles and make the 'kingdom' a reality in their lives. For lack of faith others condemned themselves to blindness.

As a source of comfort and warmth, the human dimensions of faith are not to be ignored. There is probably no more provocative image of family love and unity than that of a family gathered around a log fire. Faith is, as it were, the 'log fire' or 'hearth' of the church, where we are all 'at home'. The household of the faith has no boundaries with regard to time, space, culture, race or gender. To walk in a Cathedral, to hear a 'Kyrie' from the sixteenth century, broadcast by radio, to gaze in wonder at the stained glass windows of another age, to admire the skill that crafted the sacred vessels or embroider the altar linens, is to know oneself to be part of a family that shares the same vision and is inspired by the one faith. Faith is a gift which, transcending centuries and time zones, has the capacity to unite people of every nation and culture, race and colour in a great bond of harmonious and familial relationships centred in God.

Like the headlights of a car in a dark country lane, faith is the guiding beam which first attracts and then gathers us and guides us to the mountain of God. Centred in Christ who is 'the light of the world' our faith enables us to begin here on earth what can only be fully known and grasped in heaven, for:

'God who commanded light to shine out of darkness,
   hath shined in our hearts,
   to give knowledge of the glory of God
   in the face of Jesus' (2 Co 4:6).

Cognitive conversion

The first step to union with God, which is the goal of conversion, is belief in God's existence, for we cannot be united with one of whom we know nothing. As the author of Hebrews expresses it,

> 'No one reaches God's presence
>   until he has learned to believe' (Heb 11:6).

Conversion, therefore, begins with conviction, which is, in the first instance, an intellectual conviction that God exists and as creator of the universe and all that lives is worthy of all honour, praise and glory.

The intellectual awareness or conviction we have of God's presence comes to us by God's design and grace, for if God had not chosen to reveal himself to us there is no way in which we could come a knowledge of him or know anything of his existence. In the epistle to the Hebrews we read that,

> 'Only faith can ... prove the existence of the realities that at present remain unseen' (11:1).

Or, as another translation expresses it,

> 'Faith is the evidence of things that appear not'.

In other words, without the self-revelation of God and the gift of faith which adapts our intellectual faculty to respond to the communication of God's self there is no possibility that we could come to know God. Faith is, in fact, the only evidence we have of God's existence.

The effect of having our intellect enlightened by Divine revelation and the gift of faith is to awaken in us a new dimension of reality beyond that which the senses can perceive or the intellect project within their natural capacity. Faith, which is a higher faculty than reason, by introducing us to the realm of the Divine, exposes us to a whole new dimension of truth and 'unseen realities'.

That intellectual or cognitive conversion has to do with our grasp of reality and our perception of truth is clearly recognised by Bernard Lonergan when he defines this stage of conversion as,

'A radical clarification concerning reality'.

To have our intellect enlightened by faith, is not only to know more about God, but also to know more about ourselves as created in the image of God, and to know and understand with greater clarity God's design for the universe and the ultimate meaning and purpose of life.

It may be supposed that to be awakened by faith to 'unseen realities' will cause us to look afresh and perhaps even question some of our views or perspectives in relation to the truths and realities by which we live, for just as the telescope has changed our perception of space, so faith changes our perception of truth. Therefore, it is not unreasonable to expect that the gift of faith or the 'light of revelation' will bring into focus and highlight misapprehensions that may be held in relation to reality, and consequently have a profound effect on our appreciation and perception of truth?

Truth does not change, but as our faith matures and our relationship with God develops, our perception of truth does change. This is not to imply that truth is volatile or transient, but rather to recognise its universal, eternal and dynamic qualities which prevents its being captured in one 'still frame' of human intelligence or competence. The process of being exposed to a Divine perspective of reality which is progressively assimilated by faith will force us to reconsider many of our most treasured beliefs and values.

But what is reality, what is truth? This question, which has exercised the mind of people since the world began, has never had a definitive answer which has proved satisfactory to all. Even today there are some who believe that truth is discovered in empirical data gathered by the senses, and formulated by science, which would seem to suggest that truth is the product of scientific evidence and repetitive experiments.

In opposition to this, declaring that 'truth and provability are not the same thing' others point to the universal philosophical realities of life as the doorway to truth. They recognise that though these may defy and elude scientific research and formulation, the profound but intangible realities to which we are exposed by nature, beauty, poetry and the horror of war are the warp and weft with which we weave the tapestry of life. For them truth is experienced in the drama and aesthetic appreciation of the joyful and sorrowful, painful and happy experiences of life which cannot be captured or measured in the scientist's test tube.

The enneagram also recognises that, as the mirror of reality, truth can in fact mean different things to different people. Because each individual has a different appreciation, experience and understanding of reality, the enneagram suggests that our 'truth' may be biased in accordance with the 'centre' from which we operate, thus adding psychology to reasoning as an interpreter of truth.

The fact that there are so many distinctive and divergent avenues to truth suggest that any one perspective, no matter how tenaciously defended, provides only a partial glimpse of the whole. In the following pages I wish to consider this particular experience of truth in a little more detail. The observations I make are based on an understanding of what the enneagram teaches in relation to the different perspectives of head, gut and heart personalities concerning reality.

Truth or reality in the head centre

According to the enneagram, for individuals who operate from the head centre, reality is 'to be in tune, to be in harmony' with the universe. Beginning from this premise they will naturally seek to discover the underlying principles and natural laws which govern the harmonious development of the universe as the means of being 'in tune' with their environment. To be cognisant of such knowledge is, for head personalities, to be in possession of the 'truth', in relation to life and living.

Truth rooted in the principles of harmony is, of necessity, arrived at by the observation and the accumulation of evidence regarding the existence and nature of these principles. Whilst such principles may be useful in the establishment of secure and determined boundaries within which harmonious living becomes possible, the knowledge or implementation of these principles does not of itself create harmony or lead to truth.

No one can doubt the great advantage to be had from knowing, for example, the truth or laws which govern the rules of language, science, physics, dance, music and art. To be in possession of such an accumulation of knowledge or truth is to have a readily available tried and trusted source from which to facilitate and harmonise one's own learning process. To know the underlying principles governing any discipline can effectively free each generation from the necessity of discovering the proverbial wheel and allow them to direct their energy to other useful activities.

To circumvent or deny the basic principles or rules of harmonious living is for head centred individuals the road to chaos, anarchy and possible destruction, the very thought of which fills them with fear and dejection. Their gift to society is their awareness that the discovery of and adherence to truth, as embodied in natural law and formulated by science, is essential, not only to harmonious living but also to our very survival.

However, the desire of head persons for 'harmonious' living may become so contrived and compulsed in an individual or section of society as to blind its adherents to the possible evil consequences of living solely 'by law' or by facts. The blanket application of law, irrespective of rights, may then foster a sterile and hostile environment which denies the priority of truth, and stifles individual freedom.

One disadvantage of this limited understanding of truth is that truth itself may be sacrificed and subverted to law or knowledge, and may even become equated with a collection of 'facts', which instead of facilitating growth, freedom and harmony, may stunt and destroy life. Examples from the field of sport are often quoted in this instance, and few people would argue that knowledge of the rules of football will suffice to carry the national team to international glory. The inadequacy of 'knowledge' as opposed to experience is clearly evident in this case.

This may be less evident, and consequently more dangerous in other areas of human experience. When knowledge or evidence becomes the accepted standard and measure of truth it may be supposed that the more knowledgeable a person becomes the greater access to truth they acquire. This would confine truth to the domain of the intellect, and deny access to truth that is discovered by faith.

A few years ago the media reported an incident which occurred at Heathrow. Due to mechanical failure, the parking lot barriers ceased to function and, as a consequence, motorists were forcibly delayed in leaving the airport. When eventually, after almost two hours, the barriers were raised, the attendant insisted on charging for the length of time the barriers had been out of action. Some may say 'this has nothing to do with truth', but it does say a lot about law. In my experience, many 'law abiding' individuals, fail to interpret law in a manner that allows them to discover and implement its underlying truth.

Because head centred personalities depend on personally observed evidence as their means of acquiring truth, faith in an unseen God can be very problematic for them. They are, according to the enneagram, the group for whom faith or trust in the words of another, is very difficult.

Often the only people they trust are those who have been vested with authority, because the direction and teachings of those in authority is considered to be an important avenue to truth and, as custodians of law and order, those in authority rightly receive allegiance and loyalty.

The acceptance of authority may simplify life and provide a secure framework of reference, but 'blindly' adhered to authority can also eliminate the capacity of individuals to think for themselves and so facilitate and promote a state of dictatorship. Such a situation does not serve harmony or truth, and is in fact a denial of both. The call for a 'benevolent' dictatorship that is sometimes voiced by those who are dependent on authority is understandable, but sad. Dictatorship, which is a denial of both harmony and truth, can never be benevolent.

Reliance on authority, which is characteristic of head centred people may make them hesitant to accept new teachings, insights or customs, even those promoted by legitimate authority. Because of the sense of loyalty they have to established authority and custom, they may be very reluctant or hesitant to embrace new ideas, and any change of direction may cause them to 'panic' and withdraw their normal pattern of loyal behaviour. In 'blindness' they may refuse to accept any new interpretation or understanding of revealed truth. How many devoted and loyal members of the Roman Catholic Church still struggle with changes in the liturgy that were introduced by the Second Vatican Council?

In their desire for harmony head centred individuals may settle for regimentation, and settle for the means rather than the end. Should this happen they may fail to discover the truth which is the only legitimate goal of law. The discovery of truth will always lead to harmonious living, but law may not always lead to truth.

Truth or reality in the gut centre

For gut centred personalities reality or truth is discovered in essence, which presumes existence or being. The possession of life is for them the one great and undeniable reality, and authenticity rather than knowledge is that which gives them access to truth. In God essence and existence are identical.

Quality is a clue to authenticity, and I find it interesting that many of my friends who have identified themselves as gut personalities share a preoccupation with the quality or 'purity' of what they and I wear. 'I like your jumper, is it pure wool?' they will ask, or it may be that pure silk, pure cotton, or real leather is the object of their enquiry. No one has yet asked me if I'm wearing 'pure nylon', an indication I presume that 'purity' or quality is reserved for natural fibres, and may not be applied to those created by science.

Purity of source is, then, an important element of reality or authenticity for gut personalities, and according to the enneagram this is particularly so for them in what pertains to family roots. Legitimacy of birth as the means of preserving the 'purity' of the family or race, is given high priority. Taken to extremes, we are currently witnessing how the demand for racial purity or authenticity can lead to such crimes as so called 'ethnic cleansing'. In their search for truth, gut personalities need to examine and discover the quality and essence of being.

When I asked some of my gut centred friends to share with me their understanding of truth, all without exception, started by defining truth negatively in such terms as 'Truth is not falsehood, it is not lies, it is not devious or partial, truth is not doubtful or questionable, it is not fictitious'. Only slowly and hesitantly did they eventually come to a definition of truth as being intrinsically flawless, whole, perfect, noble and perhaps even absolute. To me their definition of truth had a pure and crystalline quality which I experience to be both fragile and strong, attractive and awesome, radical and elusive.

It is as though truth, for gut personalities, is a magic mirror which reflects back with clear, transparent accuracy the intrinsic qualities that define the very essence of being, and so provides them with the certainty and conviction of 'knowing' what is genuine or false, right or wrong, good or bad. The assurance they have of knowing with certainty, gives them great confidence in their ability to judge and act with discernment and impartiality.

That gut people need to be rooted in certainty is evident in their demand for precision and accuracy in whatever they are doing or discussing. 'What exactly do you mean by that?', they will ask the unwary purveyor of what they evidently judge to be an ill-defined opinion. Even an ordinary conversation can take on the character of a cross-examination, as the gut personality seeks for an ever more precise examination and definition of the subject being discussed or debated.

The dedication with which gut personalities struggle to achieve or acquire authentic reality can chain them to a treadmill of energy absorbing mental activity. In demanding certainty as a quality of truth gut personalities seek to achieve freedom, for them to be certain is to be free, but by the same token the need to be certain may become a bitter and self-imposed enslavement. The precise definition of truth which they so relentlessly seek and demand may open the door to the evils and deceits of fundamentalism.

The human limitations of adherence to certainty as the guarantee of truth and freedom are all too obvious. In 'Wellsprings', Anthony de Mello says that 'certainty is the sin of bigots, terrorists and Pharisees'. That bigotry and fundamentalism can become the sin of gut personalities can be observed in their intolerance with those who do not espouse their particular definition of truth, or who do not give much weight to their attention to detail or preoccupation with 'purity' or perfection. Rather than freedom rooted in truth they may choose to be quagmired in an uncompromising dedication to certainty rooted in arrogance.

It is important for gut personalities to discover that

though truth will lead to authenticity it may also possibly destroy their hard won certainties.

Truth or reality in the heart centre

Truth or reality for heart centred personalities is to be in relationship and in communication with others. Beginning from this perception of reality they will naturally seek to develop or establish wholesome relationships with God, self and others. Therefore, personal integrity, sincerity and honesty are their chosen means of pursuing truth and happiness.

Honesty and sincerity in our dealings with others has always been recognised as part of true religion, and it is this 'religious and personal' understanding of truth rather than the scientific or philosophical approaches of the other two centres that underlies the particular focus of heart personalities in relation to truth.

Probably no one will question the assumption held by heart personalities that sincerity, meaning 'without wax or gloss', is a basic component of all interpersonal relationships.

In his dialogue with Nicodemus, Jesus teaches us that those who 'do' truth come to the light or to enlightenment. To 'do' truth means to bear witness to the truths we profess to believe and is an essential ingredient of religious faith. Unless we bear witness to what we believe our faith will remain sterile and void. In practical terms this means that consent to an intellectual perception of truth has no value unless or until it is validated by good works that promote good personal relationships for,

'Anyone who claims to be in the light
but hates his brother is still in the dark' (1 Jn 2:9).

In their compulsive search for understanding and wisdom heart centred individuals are often tempted to promote and enhance their 'image' to the detriment of integrity and at the expense of truth. By what are euphemistically called white lies, half-truths or tall stories they seek to embroider and embellish their accomplishment and reputation, or those of their family, in order to make themselves acceptable and valued as friends.

The ability they have to create and project an image of themselves as a means of 'acquiring friends and influencing people', is part of their stock in trade for self advancement. This desire, which springs from the need they have to impress others in order to gain friends, can be compounded when it becomes a deliberate attempt to gain an unfair advantage over others. The Bible leaves us in no doubt regarding the importance of honesty and just standards in all commercial and business negotiations,

'A false balance is an abomination to the Lord,
But a just weight is his delight' (Pr 11:1).

Strange as it may seem, heart centred people who compulsively promote self-image as a means of self-aggrandisement can become so subordinated to image as to be deceived by it when used by others. As would be expected, dependency on the power of image to influence others has the effect of dulling one's senses and perception to reality. This may explain the exaggerated and superficial values that have come to be associated with Hollywood. In giving so much importance to image it is easy to understand why they easily fall prey to the image or deceitfulness of others.

In general heart centred people, more than others, are likely to be very direct and truthful in speech. On occasion they can be embarrassingly blunt even to the point of rudeness, and will insist on calling 'a spade a spade' even when the delicacy of the matter being discussed calls for greater sensitivity.

In their desire for integrity they appear to have an almost compulsive need to strip away any shade or shadow of deceit in their relations with others, whilst at the same

'COGNITIVE CONVERSION IS TO TRUTH'
(*Lonergan*)

Any debate on the subject of truth will highlight the different perspectives from which it is perceived by different people.

As logical thinkers, HEAD centred personalities approach truth from the perspective of verifiable data.

For GUT centred people truth is about essential reality or genuine quality. It is about authenticity and reality.

For HEART centred people truth is about honesty and sincerity in personal relationships. It is about singleness of purpose and intent in dealing with others.

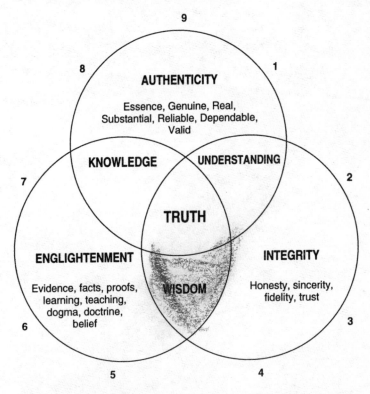

According to Christian Spirituality the gifts of knowledge, understanding and wisdom, facilitate our search for truth.

time seeking to promote the friendship by enhancing their image. It is the dilemma with which they constantly live, and is a difficult act to balance.

To speak the truth with simplicity and single-mindedness of purpose is an important facet of cognitive conversion, as it is the means by which we attain the innocence and integrity that is characteristic of the true believer. When their desire for truth and integrity is superseded by their desire for friendship heart people may settle for image, and so resist the grace of conversion.

Truth, pursued with honesty and sincerity will always enhance our integrity, but may ruthlessly expose and destroy our image.

Logical reasoning

The purpose of logical reasoning which, according to the enneagram, is used preferentially by head centred personalities is to discover truth through the enlightenment of facts and evidence. Logical thinkers pursue enlightenment and their thinking is characterised by clarity of vision and depth of insight. It is important for them to see evidence in order for them to be convinced by facts.

By a process of synthesis and induction, facts and figures, proofs and evidence are welded together by logical thinkers to construct a 'chain' of reasoning with which to argue and consolidate a particular point of view. In the opinion of Mary Helen Kelley, who places herself in this centre, head people 'learn slowly and laboriously', step by step, link by link. If a link in the chain or process of reasoning is broken or missing it is possible that logical thinkers will have difficulty in establishing connections with other relevant data.

Their dependence on structured thinking becomes evident in the care with which logicians organise their facts in telling a story or giving a lecture. In this situation it becomes evident how important it is for them to get the facts or events in correct sequence in order for them to have confidence in presenting their material, as any interruption which breaks their line of thought may be for them a cause of great confusion.

Because logical thinkers experience life at the 'head' level, they acquire knowledge mostly by observation and perception. Facts and figures, proofs and evidence, formula and syntax, instructions and rules are important to them, as being verifiable norms, which give structure and support to their logical approach to life.

The logical process of head thinkers which, as mentioned previously, is sometimes spoken of as a chain of reasoning or a train of thoughts, would seem to imply a certain facility or flexibility in this type of thinking. In reality, the accumulation of data which is crucial to logical thought may become foundational to the construction of a deeply entrenched wall which eliminates any possibility of movement in their thinking.

Constructed of evidence, proofs and facts, in place of bricks and mortar, when complete the wall or edifice so constructed may become a fortress of protection and defence against conviction. Such a defence system then becomes part of the logical thinker's foundation of reality and of relating to the world. If, for some reason, logical thinkers hold a 'truth' that is ill founded, it is then possible that they may become 'blinded' by their own reasoning and effectively cut off from truth.

Oddly enough, it is the logical thinker, whose reasoning is founded on the perception and examination of evidence and the deduction of truth from evidence, who is likely to neglect, overlook, or even deny evidence that is contrary to what they already believe. When the true logical thinker holds tenets that are marginal at best, clear, indisputable evidence presented by others may fail to convince them. They may become very argumentative in defence of their own evidence and observations and the importance of proving their belief structure and of appearing to be more knowledgeable than others may then surface.

Resistance to any truth but their own and to any light or evidence not self generated can cause head people to become argumentative and dogmatic. When this happens, the important thing for them is no longer to discover truth, but to be proved right in their argument and to be recognised as more knowledgeable than others.

In a sense this reaction should be expected, because the logical thinker's foundation of truth and being are threatened by new evidence from an outsider. Examples of this reaction are common, from the domestic scene to the international scientific world, from the trivia to the essential. Even when the issue being contested is insignificant and lacks importance, it may be defended with a vehemence which not only generates more heat than light but is actually resistant to truth. In 'defeat' the logical thinker may exhibit a miserly surrender to the truth. To say that their acquiescence may lack generosity and sincerity, may well be an understatement of the fact.

How, we may ask does this relate to conversion? As stated earlier, the purpose of logical reasoning is to discover truth through the examination of evidence and facts. However, as we have seen, such thinkers can be threatened in day to day living by the existence of new knowledge. The challenge presented to logical thinkers by new evidence may impede their openness to new frontiers and horizons of knowledge, and so dull their intellect in relation to truth.

That this same attitude may influence their acceptance of faith is evident in the words of Jesus to Nicodemus:

'If you do not believe me
when I speak about things in this world,
how are you going to believe me
when I speak to you about heavenly things?'

(Jn 3:12).

The willingness to own the limitations of our reasoning abilities, to refuse to build walls constructed of facts and be willing to follow the light from whichever source it comes is the only sure way to find truth.

If the logical thinker is not open to truth or light in daily living and in interpersonal relationships, then it may be expected that this same attitude will prevail in relation to Divine revelation. If at the level of logic we close ourselves to ascertainable facts, just how receptive can we hope to be to the mystery of eternal truth revealed to us in the person of Christ? When John's disciples enquired of Jesus,

SYMBOLS OF LOGICAL REASONING

The purpose of logical reasoning is to accumulate evidence that will validate or 'clinch' an argument.

By a process of synthesis logical reasoning seeks to acquire a comprehensive variety of data with which to extend knowledge and dispel ignorance.

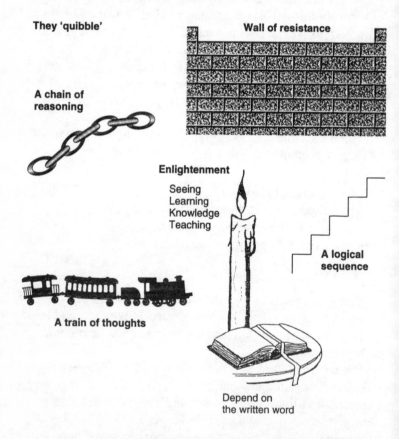

They 'quibble'

Wall of resistance

A chain of reasoning

Enlightenment

Seeing
Learning
Knowledge
Teaching

A logical sequence

A train of thoughts

Depend on the written word

Generally speaking logic is a process of enlightenment and growing awareness of truth but used defensively it may become a wall of resistance that is impervious to truth.

'Rabbi, where do you live?' the invitation was,
'Come and see'.

Had they been cocooned in their own little world behind
a barricade of facts they may never have discovered the
true Light.

Only when enlightened by the Gift of Knowledge can
the human intellect discover the truths of God.

The gift of knowledge

One important aspect of human psychology highlighted by the enneagram is that we appear to have an almost self-destructive perversity which continually thwarts or impedes the fulfilment of our desires. Though we may like to consider ourselves as 'rational beings' we often deviate from what is reasonable, in such a way as to make it appear that we are seeking the very opposite of what is desired. That this strangely deviant behaviour is characteristic would seem to suggest that it is by nature compulsive and hidden. St Paul writes graphically of this as a personal experience in his letter to the Romans:

> '...instead of doing the good things I want to do,
> I carry out the sinful things I do not want' (7:9).

That the enneagram graphically indicates numerous and various ways in which people fall into this deviant behaviour is, I believe, one of its merits as a tool of spiritual growth.

To redeem and free us from this self-destructive pattern of behaviour we receive in conversion, in addition to the theological virtues of faith, hope and charity, the gifts of the Holy Spirit. These gifts, traditionally named as wisdom, understanding, counsel, fortitude, knowledge, piety and fear of the Lord, are the means by which our minds, hearts and souls are alerted to the 'irrationality' of our chosen way of 'being' and are opened to God's way of being. By these gifts faith is enlightened, hope is confirmed, charity is perfected, and goodness is attained. They are the channels of grace by which God moulds us and makes us docile to the inspirations of his grace.

In the early years of my Christian formation I was presented with a knowledge of the faith which defined it as being a divinely motivated and infused assent to revealed truth. The basic principle concerning faith was that it was a 'body' of doctrine which, though beyond human understanding, was guaranteed by God to be true. Faith was presented to me as knowledge about doctrine, dogma and truth about God who seemed quite remote.

Away from school I experienced another dimension of faith which was all about love, trust, security and Divine providence. God apparently lived in my home and, although I could not see him with physical sight, his presence was imminent and pervasive. My mother not only spoke to us about God, she talked to God about us and harnessed his goodness and love on our behalf. Faith was about our poverty and God's richness.

These two different aspects of faith, knowledge about God and relationship with God, clarify in my mind the difference between a purely intellectual understanding of faith, and a faith that has been ignited and set aglow by the Holy Spirit's gift to us of knowledge. By transporting faith from the head to the heart, the Gift of knowledge leads us to understand the truth concerning the things of this world in relationship to God. It weans our minds and hearts from everything that is not God and makes us poor in spirit and hungry and thirsty for the things of God.

A few years ago I attended a series of lectures given by Fr John Sheets, Auxilliary Bishop of the Diocese of Fort Wayne. In these lectures he spoke to us of Christ:

'The king who became servant,
the priest who became victim,
the shepherd who became a lamb.'

Everything that Christ teaches us about the ways of God reveals to us the vanity of human perception and the impotency of human logic. Faith it would appear turns logic upside down. If, in our struggle to be 'right' we are accustomed to resist logic which is so 'reasonable' and evident, how will we be able to contend with a faith which is so unreasonable and hidden. Could it be that 'we have eyes and do not see' until our worldly perception of truth has been 'dismantled and abolished' by the Holy Spirit?

Hope

At the end of World War II, when the ending of hostilities appeared to be in sight, there suddenly appeared over the skies of southern England a new and fearsome weapon known as the V1. These pilotless planes or unmanned rockets were, in ridicule, initially called doodle-bugs, but once their lethal potential became known, those in the firing line began to refer to them as the 'Bob Hope' bombs. This name arose from the experience that when the sound of their engine suddenly ceased, giving a warning of their imminent fall, the most prudent line of defence was to 'bob and hope'.

'Where there is life there is hope' is a popular saying which reminds us that no one can survive without hope, especially in times of life-threatening danger. At such times it is often the 'expectation and desire' of being rescued that ensures the happy solution to the disaster, because the faintest glimmer of hope has power to engage the energy of the victim in a creative struggle for survival. Even in less dramatic moments when we are merely struggling with the hum-drum tenor of life we may be tempted to escape into that fantasy land of dreams and desires which, for people of my generation, exists 'somewhere over the rainbow'.

Hope, 'the desire and search for future good', is the virtue that keeps us cheerful in the midst of doubt and danger and gives us the assurance that things will improve, life will go on, and freedom will be ours. By focusing our attention on the 'silver lining' that reflects the glory behind the cloud, hope enables us to enjoy in the present the certainty of a rosy future.

The theological virtue of hope is also eschatological or future orientated in that it looks forward in joyful expectation to eternal life with God in the possession of heaven. Theological hope, unlike natural hope, is not mere 'wishful thinking' but a confident belief, rooted in the Word of God, that heaven is our rightful home and will be ours if we follow in the footsteps of Jesus.

To preserve the life we have and live ever more fully is a natural human instinct. The symbols of hope used in the liturgy all direct our attention to the fulfilment of this natural desire for life and happiness which are offered to us by God. The rainbow that reflects the presence of the sun in clouded skies and the anchor providing security in stormy seas each hold in sign the promise and assurance of God's imminent and saving presence in times of discouragement and doubt. For the Christian there can be no greater sign and promise of new life in the midst of death than that of Easter, which reveals to us in splendour God's power and desire to save and recreate us anew in the image of his Son Jesus.

Of ourselves, we have no reason to hope, because nothing we can do or achieve by our own merits can earn for us eternal life. Life comes to us as a gift from others not only at the moment of birth, but in the daily struggle to survive, and just as we are dependent on others for the gift and maintenance of natural life, so also are we dependent on God for the gift of eternal life.

The experience of dependency on others for the attainment and maintenance of life can have adverse effects on relationships both human and Divine. In the human situation there is always the possibility that we may have 'merited' the assistance of others, not so with God, because no matter what we achieve or do we are always in God's debt. Doubt in our own worth may then cause us to despair of God's love, or, at the opposite extreme, may cause us to engage in a relentless pursuit of 'perfection' in order to merit his love. The theological virtue of hope frees us from the ravages of such extremes of despair and presumption by assuring us of God's unconditional love, and by predisposing us to seek only what God desires in our regard.

In his letter to Titus Paul clearly spells out for us the source and foundation of our hope:

> 'But when the goodness and love of God our saviour for mankind were revealed, it was not because he was concerned with any righteous actions we might have done ourselves; it was for no reason except his own compassion that he saved us' (Ti 3:4,5).

Contrary to what human prudence dictates or to how the world judges, we learn from this text that it is weakness and not virtue or excellence which attracts the saving acts of God on our behalf. Our need and infirmity, which can never exceed God's compassion, is the measure of hope, just as the goodness and power of God is its principle and foundation.

To hope in God is to share in his compassion and love for the world, and to be a witness to the kingdom that is to come. Firm hope in God will make us strong and courageous in facing the trials and tribulations that are an ingredient of human life, and will be a constant reminder that:

> 'We have not here a lasting city,
> but we look for one that is to come.'

Moral conversion

We each have a story and a dream, and God is the author of both. The dream that God has for each of us is that we should inherit eternal life by being transformed into the image of his son Jesus. Our dream is to become like God. Unfortunately, we sometimes seek the fulfilment of our dream in pursuits and activities that destroy rather than transform our lives, and thus negate our dream, but we can never negate God's dream. By the grace of conversion God invites us to change the focus of our search for fulfilment and by attracting us to the Divine goodness made visible in Christ, empowers us to realise and live both dreams.

To be attracted by the Divine goodness to the extent that we desire to become good and are willing to suffer the pain of change and transformation is, according to Bernard Lonergan, the grace of moral conversion. This suggests that in the process of moral conversion we are given the grace and ability to discern the nature and character of goodness and to recognise the lack of it in our lives.

By definition, 'moral' is concerned with the character and disposition of a person in relation to the distinction between right and wrong. Thus a person may be judged to be 'moral' or 'good' according to the traits of character and dispositions he or she exhibits. God is good or moral by nature, we become so by grace. By putting us in touch with the goodness of God, made manifest to us in Christ, moral conversion alerts us to a whole new dimension and quality of life that, if embraced with courage and determination, will ensure our transformation, our eternal happiness.

Goodness, which is the object of morality, can be difficult to define, which makes it a popular subject of debate. For those who believe in absolute morality and look to it for standardised definitions of right and wrong, the moral relativism of others can appear to be a denial of objective values and a surrender to anarchy. Who is right and who is wrong? The reality is that whichever attitude we adopt or option we choose decides our standard of morality, and establishes the values by which we decide to live. No one lives with a judgement-free morality.

Morality then is about standards and judgement in relation to value and worth which, according to circumstances or situations, may be objective or subjective. Space travel has taught us, if we had not already grasped it, that in order to weigh or value anything we must have a centre of gravity as it is impossible to weigh anything in space. Gravity is that which gives weight to an object.

In attempting to make sound and valid judgements which will be to our advantage we frequently have to engage in a process of discernment in which we compare and contrast, for example, black and white, good or bad, sour or sweet. The questions to be asked will differ according to the subject of the judgement, but the process will be the same.

One of the difficulties we face in making a judgement is first to establish our centre of gravity in relation to the subject of the discernment, for in the absence of gravity the judgement will lack the intrinsic qualities of value and worth. In buying a car, or choosing a holiday venue this may be relatively easy, but in the question of morality or goodness it can be very difficult. To truly discern or judge the morality of our actions our judging scales must first be 'earthed' in Divine goodness.

In making moral judgements I believe that the theological virtue of hope is our God-centred point of gravity. The attainment of heaven and life eternal is both the object of hope and the goal and purpose of our moral decisions. Unless we are rooted in Christ, our moral decisions may be warped by the lack of goodness within us, and be no more than a subjective judgement in which self-interest holds the controlling card. Wrong, then becomes right, deceit becomes truth and death becomes life.

The theological virtue of hope does, I believe, inform our faculty of judgement in relation to goodness in the manner in which faith enlightens the intellect in relation to truth. To be anchored to God by the theological virtue of hope is to know with certainty where life is to be found, and it is in the search for life that we discover goodness.

Many events are recorded in the scriptures in which the beauty of God's presence and the radiance of his being are manifest in an external manifestation of glory. The goodness of God is so vibrant and powerful that it cannot be hidden or contained but exposes itself in glory. By the grace of moral conversion we are invited and adopted to participate in God's goodness and so reflect the splendour of his glory.

In the Bible the word 'glory' is used in reference to weight or value and, by implication, bears witness to the worth, dignity or goodness of a person, object or event. Glory does not create goodness but is the external manifestation or emanation that exposes goodness to view. Because it is intrinsically linked with goodness, glory may on occasion be mistaken for goodness and be sought independently of goodness.

Because God is essentially good, glory is a natural phenomenon of his presence. That glory also attaches itself to human goodness, is attested to by that feeling of inner radiance and joy which gives us a sense of wholeness and satisfaction when we perform a good action. The suffusion of warmth and glow in the depth of our being on these occasions is tangible evidence and assurance of the weight or worth of our actions, giving rise to the proverb,

'Virtue is its own reward.'

To perceive the glory of God, that is to be confronted by God's innate goodness or moral attributes, is to be exposed to our sinfulness or lack of goodness. In the Bible the phrases 'give glory to God' and 'confess your sins' mean the same thing, because to experience the goodness of God

80

is to know and recognise our own lack of goodness. An example of this is provided by St Peter on the occasion of the miraculous catch of fish, when the wonder of the miracle forced him to his knees in acknowledgement of his sinfulness (cf Lk 5:1-11).

The Gospel recounts numerous other occasions when people who had met Jesus, 'the radiant light of God's glory' were fired with a desire to be made 'whole'. In his 'glorious' presence they were aware of what was lacking in their own lives and looked to him for healing. This is what happens to those who encounter God in grace, they are simultaneously filled with a yearning for healing and a desire for wholeness or perfection that is rooted in the goodness and holiness of God.

From this we can deduce that morality and worship are inextricably bound and that we do in fact 'worship what we value' or whatever we perceive and judge to be good. As stated previously, the theological virtue of hope which directs our attention to the attainment of eternal life does, I believe, inform our judgement in relation to genuine worth and value.

When our judgement is informed and enriched by the gift of hope we are able to recognise and discern the presence of goodness and as a result we live with an awesome respect for the 'worthiness' of God's self and God's people. This respect, which is rooted in a God-inspired appreciation of goodness, is the very wellspring of moral conversion and worship.

Important aspects of both worship and morality is that they commit us to live with justice and respect for the rights of others. That worship and morality have to do with justice and, therefore, with right relationship is clearly evident from the well known and often quoted words of Micah,

'What is good has been explained to you, man:
this is what Yahweh asks of you:
only this, to act justly,

81

to love tenderly
and to walk humbly with your God' (Micah 6:8).

This text of Micah which speaks with such clarity and simplicity of the nature of goodness, leaves us in no doubt that to be good or 'moral' is to recognise, appreciate and show due respect for the rights of God, others, self and nature. To live in such a manner, with due regard for others, at peace with God and in justice with our neighbours, demands of us a self-denying love which cuts at the very roots of our innate selfishness.

In the Gospel we discover God incarnate in the person of Jesus, inviting us to accept the challenge to live, and think and love in a new and better way. By submitting our lives to the example and teaching of Jesus and to the teaching of the Gospel we discover within ourselves and society those things that need to be transformed or changed 'for the better'. The experience of God's goodness made manifest and available in Christ is, therefore, the motivation and dynamic source of moral conversion.

That our Christian vocation is to be conformed to the image of Christ is confirmed by St Paul,

'Before the world was made,
he chose us, chose us in Christ
to be holy and spotless,
and to live through love in his presence,
determining that we should be his adopted sons,
through Jesus Christ' (Eph 1:4,5).

From this text we learn that moral conversion is a process of personal transformation which, initiated by God, prepares us to participate in God's own life of holiness and love, through the merits of Christ. By the grace of moral conversion our heart is inclined towards good, our intellect is informed with regard to good, and our will is activated to choose good, and so we are fitted by grace to grow into the image of God's own son, Jesus.

It would seem that there is no end to the extent and scope of moral conversion. Wonder, worth, and worship; respect and awe; justice and justification; discernment and judgement; holiness and transformation; each and all are related to the recognition, appreciation and attainment of goodness, and are a participation in the morality and goodness of God.

Because of the wide scope of morality it is not to be wondered that different people have widely different appreciation of goodness. As with truth the question 'what is goodness?' may never be definitively answered to the satisfaction of everyone.

Turning to the teaching of the enneagram we see that head, gut and heart personalities are considered to operate from distinctly different sets of values. This suggests to me that each triad of personalities has a different concept of what constitutes goodness and therefore a distinct approach to morality.

In the following pages I intend to look at the values given priority by each of the triads in an attempt to understand the manner in which their value system may influence their approach to morality. I hasten to add that as we move out of our preferred centre, and live integratedly from head gut and heart, which is of course the desired goal of self-knowledge, our appreciation of goodness becomes less fragmented, and consequently more focused and integrated.

Moral conversion in the head centre

Harmony, according to the enneagram, constitutes goodness for head centred personalities. Their need to be 'in tune' with their environment and 'in step' with the norms and expectations of society leads them to value law as the means of attaining an ordered, well regulated and harmonious manner of living. People in this centre have a need to be 'right' and seek to achieve this by conformity to the norms and laws of society. Head personalities are sticklers for rules, if there is not a rule 'make one', they seem to say, ' then we will all know what to do and can live in peace'. This desire for structure and uniformity springs from their desire for harmony, but denies the inherent quality of harmony as a pleasing combination of different and distinct elements. Such persons might be said to have a law centred morality.

Though it would be presumptuous to suggest that head personalities do not distinguish between law and morality I believe it is important to establish the boundaries of law in relation to morality, and to recognise that legality and morality are not synonymous.

Looking at Genesis 8:22 we learn that,

'As long as earth lasts,
sowing and reaping,
cold and heat,
summer and winter,
day and night shall cease no more.'

From this we may deduce that whatever God does he does consistently. That is to say our God is reliable and dependable, one might even say predictable. His constancy and faithfulness are so consistent that they take on the nature of law, which in this sense refers to the abiding characteristic of God's faithfulness and love.

Freedom and security are the underlying principle and purpose of all natural and Divine law. The 'invariable phenomenon' which is characteristic of natural laws provides a secure and consistent framework of reference in our understanding of the universe. Such, too, is the nature of God's love for us, because his love is so dependable we know that we will never be abandoned or rejected. More stable than the laws of physics, God's love is predictable and will never change.

A second definition of 'law' refers to the rules and customs by which a society is governed or regulated. In every society certain rules are recognised as binding on the whole community. The purpose of such rules is to establish set norms and acceptable patterns of behaviour which will allow people to live together in harmony with due consideration for the rights of others. In theory these laws will follow the precedent of 'natural' law and will seek to facilitate and enhance life by providing a framework of freedom and security. If it should happen that laws are arbitrary and capricious they cannot serve this purpose and must be resisted.

Once promulgated, civic rules are enforced by lawful authority. The limitation of such law is that it is confined to what is negative rather than what is positive. For example law can impose a curfew on noise, but it cannot enforce peace; it may prohibit murder but it cannot command love. At most, civic law can establish a legal code of practice which provides for basic security and legislates for the punishment of offences.

That the inherent limitations of imposed law are not always recognised, and may be seriously misunderstood, is evident when legality becomes confused with morality. Law is then promoted as the source and fountain of justification, goodness and morality, and is accorded an authority and responsibility which it does not possess. To confuse legality with morality is to imply that legislation is sufficient to form a moral person or produce a moral society. Though law may impose a framework of order it cannot, of itself, engender life, freedom or justification. This I think is an important distinction, especially for head personalities for whom law and order have high priority and value.

In a really compulsed state the head personality can enforce what is often a false 'harmony' into every area of life. I remember once seeing a library in which the books had been colour coded according to size, and were kept under lock and key. This may be an extreme case, but it is not rare, especially in this who 'live by the law'. This sort of compulsed regimentation which masquerades as harmony, lacks the basic principles of natural and Divine law.

Morality, which is gifted to us by God, is a commitment to goodness, and life is the greatest goodness God can give. It is love, not law, which engenders life, and as the most potent force of harmonisation in creation, is the essence of Christian life. To be controlled by law is to be diminished as a person. According to St Paul we do not live by law but by grace (cf Rom 6:15). Grace generates law, it does not follow it.

There may be those who say that love is an easy 'cop out', because they fail to recognise that when love dominates all is lawful, all is harmonious. Harmony and love have to be worked at, but regimentation and law can be blueprinted with no regard for people. It may be possible to end the day knowing that our observance of the law has been flawless, not so with love. The nature of love is to extend our horizons beyond anything we ever dare aspire to and will always challenge us to go that extra mile, to make that extra effort. We may pride ourselves on our observance of the law, but in the ways of love we will always be learners.

Moral conversion invites us to be transformed by goodness. This demands that we examine our priorities and values. In making harmonious living their highest good, head personalities are in touch with the desire and need of all people to live within a framework of security and freedom. Their concern for peace and harmony is a gift that enriches everyone. However, when law becomes an end rather than a means it destroys the very harmony that it desires to promote, and enslaves people in a treadmill of lifeless regimentation and conformity.

At the transfiguration of Jesus, Moses and Elijah stood as witnesses to the power of Law rooted in justice and love to transform individuals and society. However, in the absence of mutual love, even the law of Sinai was powerless to effect transformation. Only with the coming of Christ who won for us the gift of a 'new heart' were we brought into the harmonious relationships which, by freeing us from chaos and fear, established us in security and harmony.

Moral conversion in the gut centre

For gut people goodness is synonymous with life in all its fullness and richness of expression. Because, for them, life without freedom is meaningless they willingly engage in a life long struggle to achieve and maintain control of their own destiny. They appear to recognise and accept that their need to survive and be free will be constantly challenged by the vicissitudes of life and seem destined to be held in tension between the extremes of life and death, victory and defeat, freedom and control.

Their need to be in control of their lives and destiny will naturally raise for them the question of how best to achieve freedom, whatever the circumstances. To be certain appears to be an important avenue to freedom for them and is achieved by their demand for precision and accuracy in whatever information pertains to their needs.

Practise is another trusted escape route to freedom. Let me explain. In order to accomplish anything worthwhile dedication is necessary. Freedom to play a musical instrument, drive a car, paint a masterpiece or set a world record for sprinting is achieved by dedication and practise. No one, no matter how talented, performs a double axle spin the first time they take to the ice.

According to the enneagram, gut personalities, who equate goodness with freedom, appear to have an innate capacity for dedication and commitment to an ideal. Recognised by the enneagram as people of 'habit', repetition comes easily to them and facilitates the desire they apparently have to attain 'perfection' in all that they do. In the accomplishment of their desire to excel they are prepared to spend long hours of tedious practise, in the awareness, no doubt, that 'practise makes perfect'.

To say that we become free by practise is not to deny that no amount of practise will compensate for lack of talent. An essential aspect of personal freedom is the ability to recognise limitations and discern possibilities. Noted as they are for the manner in which they painstakingly consider and weigh pros and cons before making a decision, this too is a gift for which gut personalities appear to have a natural gift.

Because gut personalities tend to equate 'perfection' with their particular understanding of goodness they may feel threatened by anything which could be considered to harm their reputation, family honour or self esteem. For them reputation is power, power is might and might is right. It is not difficult to find examples of individuals and groups who operate from such a biased and elitist perception of morality, and confuse the achievement of merit, excellence or the circumstances of birth, with goodness.

This leads us back to the suggestion made above, that glory, which is the visible manifestation of goodness, may influence our pursuit of goodness. It is possible that gut personalities who pursue excellence with such commitment and ardour may seek glory independently from its source, in such a way that the attainment of excellence and merit may be accorded a moral dimension it does not possess, and so becomes a substitute for goodness.

We all love glory. Unfortunately we sometimes seek it in isolation from the goodness of which it is a sign. A few hours of television viewing will suffice to show us the way in which advertisers 'glorify' sex, strength, beauty, talent and food in an attempt to give them a weight or worth which they do not possess. Even violence is glorified, and, in spite of all evidence to the contrary, war continues to be projected as a contest of merit, an arena of glory.

In the fields of sport and entertainment, finance and politics, religion and education, medals and awards are eagerly sought as a proof and recognition of merit. As long as these awards are recognised for what they are, a record of achievement, all may be well. However, when trophies are revered as signs of 'perfection', and achievements are substituted for honour, then we are in danger of 'worshipping false values', which is a definition of idolatry.

The fervour with which trophies and awards are sought and promoted as signs of goodness, worth, merit, is not lessened by the fact that they are often recognised for what they are. 'Trappings of glory' they may be called, but are nevertheless sought after and valued.

According to the enneagram gut personalities are those who are most likely to be concerned with reputation and honour, i.e. glory. By nature and grace they are endowed with a plethora of gifts which enable them to excel in sport, music, language, dance and leadership. In this centre of balance and habit, excellence and perfection are pursued with energy and single-mindedness of purpose. Gut personalities tend to be highly critical of anything second best, and are not shy in setting themselves up as judge and jury of the achievements of themselves and others.

It is not difficult to understand that such personalities, so richly endowed, may readily seek to focus on their achievements as indisputable signs of excellence. That the achievements are considered to be a reason for self-glorification is to misunderstand the nature of glory and, therefore, of goodness, and to pursue glory for its own sake in isolation from morality, is to misunderstand both the nature of glory and the nature of goodness.

Moral conversion in the gut centre awakens us to the reality that we have nothing of ourselves in which we may glory, but receive everything, even life itself, from God. It is by using the gift of life to its full capacity, for goodness, that we both glorify and are glorified by God for, according to St Irenaeus,

'The glory of God is that people should be fully alive.'

This, what gut personalities wish for most of all, is the aim and goal of moral conversion.

Moral conversion in the heart centre

The greatest value or goodness for heart centred personalities is the achievement of self-realisation through the

89

discovery of personal identity. By our use of the personal adjective in such phrases as 'my sister', 'my son', 'my parents', 'my cousin', we do not hesitate to claim others as our own and to recognise that we belong to a family and know ourselves within the context of a particular network of personal relationships. Relationships which hold the key to our identity are, therefore, of vital concern to those who operate from this centre.

Because of the priority given to relationships by heart centred personalities, it is important for them to have healthy, wholesome and what might be considered 'privileged' relationships. It can, therefore, be important for them to know and mix with what they consider to be the 'right set' as this gives them a sense of their own worth and dignity. According to their understanding, friendship, association or identification with others are a proclamation of who we recognise ourselves to be. By being seen in the 'right company' heart personalities hope to achieve success and make themselves acceptable, approved and valued by the social group to which they belong.

Geared to success heart personalities have a tendency to foster advantageous alliances and friendships as a means of self-aggrandisement, and are most likely to seek goodness in privilege. This may give rise to a morality that is rooted in human respect, the 'what will the neighbours say?' syndrome.

As a society we build 'tabernacles' and 'temples' to the gods of success, and surround them with an aura of pretentious elitism in the vain hope of conferring greatness and worth, i.e. goodness. Exclusive clubs with their protected membership list may also attempt to foster the illusion of endowing with value and worth their carefully selected patrons. In their desire for quality experience and appreciation of 'class' heart personalities may relish the opportunity of patronising such venues.

This is not to suggest that quality experiences are to be avoided as though morally tainted. The point I wish to make is that some people attempt to bolster or promote their goodness or worth by their association and membership of exclusive clubs or groups, in what may be referred to as the 'High Society' syndrome. That such a hope is doomed to failure from the start is not always evident to those who think this way. Once again, it is an example of poor judgement in relation to the nature and quality of goodness. Heart personalities, according to the enneagram, are those who are most likely to be taken in by appearances, and to confuse quality as a standard of moral superiority.

In the presence of the socially or educationally 'elite', heart personalities may be tempted to echo the sentiments of Peter on the occasion of the Transfiguration.

'Lord, it is wonderful for us to be here, so let us make three tents, one for you, one for Moses and one for Elijah' (Mk 9:5,6).

Justification by association. I am good because I know and am recognised by the people who matter. This is the stumbling block for heart centred personalities, who frequently seem to equate goodness with privilege, class and culture.

In accordance with their desire and need to acquire 'quality' in their relationships, image, appearance, presentation, name, title and role, may also become values of great importance to them as symbols of identification with a particular group. The television programme 'Keeping up Appearances' gives a parody of these attitudes and values in the life of the eccentric and snobbish Hyacinth Bouquet.

The use of image as a statement of personal identity loses its purpose when image becomes a means of identification with a particular group. Instead of being a proclamation of personal integrity it becomes a means of claiming association with a desirable set. An example of this is seen by the manner in which people are influenced by prevailing fashion and will conform to its demands whether or not it suits their individual requirements.

Their desire to belong, to be seen in the right company,

to be befriended by the right class, to circulate in the right circles, makes them sensitive to the opinion of others. That the fear of risking censure, or 'losing face', may cause them to lack moral courage at the expense of personal integrity is an indication of the poor judgement they exhibit in relation to goodness. They recognise their need for companionship, and appreciate the value of true friendship and integrity, but are willing to sacrifice time and perhaps even talent to mix with those whom they may envy rather than admire. That they do this unconsciously does not lessen or weaken their ambition.

The desire and hope to attain goodness by association with the 'right' people, is a very denial of the nature of human persons who, as Christians, we believe are created in the image and likeness of God. It may give rise to a morality based on the concept of privilege rather than goodness and that is person rather than God-centred. This also is subtle form of idolatry. This is not to suggest that it is wrong to limit or contain our 'circle of friendship' because at some level this is to recognise the limitation of our human condition. The fault lies in living with a self-centred and false set of values, that is a denial of the inherent dignity of each person.

To summarise, moral conversion is to goodness. Arriving at goodness can be very difficult as it implies the ability to discern and judge correctly the value and worth of whatever promotes or negates the attainment of goodness. In looking at conversion in the three centres of the enneagram I have tried to indicate the various ways in which judgement and discernment in relation to goodness may be limited by different personalities.

Head personalities value law as the means of attaining harmony and order which for them constitutes goodness. In doing so they may be in danger of substituting regimentation for law and of becoming like automated tin soldiers, incapable of independent thought and action. Their dependence on, and misunderstanding of law may prevent their recognising the basic human right of freedom.

'MORAL CONVERSION IS TO GOOD'
(*Lonergan*)

Moral conversion is about the discernment and recognition of worth. It is about values apprehended and pursued, as the means of attaining life.

According to the enneagram, HEAD centred personalities value *harmony* or *syntony* as their highest good, GUT centred personalities value *homeostasis* or *balance* and *equilibrium* as the means of achieving life and freedom which is their highest good and HEART centred people discover goodness in warm and loving *relationships*.

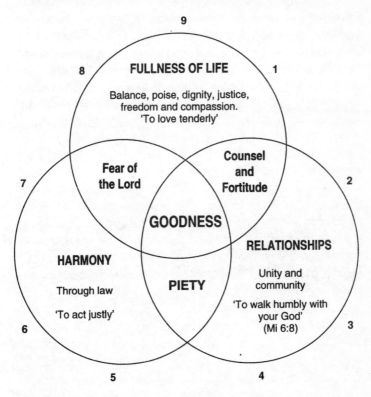

In Christian Spirituality it is recognised that Fear of the Lord, Counsel, Fortitude and Piety are the gifts of the Holy Spirit which facilitate our pursuit of morality.

Gut people value excellence, merit and glory as the means of attaining freedom. They desire not only to be 'perfect' but to be recognised as such. Their desire for perfection and hunger for glory leads them to value and equate self-glorification with goodness. They often consider themselves to be models of 'perfection' and paragons of 'virtue' and have the medals and certificates to prove it. It is possible that their morality is based on the promotion of their reputation and honour, rather than on justice and right living.

People in the heart centre consider that goodness is attained by identification with the socially successful. For this reason they value association with the rich, learned, powerful and famous as the means of attaining personal worth and of conferring personal dignity. The promotion of self-image as a means of self-aggrandisement may prevent their recognising and attaining true goodness. The division of society into 'desirables and undesirables' may alienate them from the God who is the source of all goodness and the centre of all being.

Analogical reasoning

The purpose of analogical reasoning is to evaluate, weigh and consider information in order to make correct and viable judgements in relation to important decisions. By definition analogical reasoning is precise, measured and balanced. Through a process of reasoning from parallel cases and past experiences and through tracing resemblances, making comparisons and noting contrasts, analogical reasoning comes to fruition in judgement about what 'ought' to be.

This type of reasoning is the means whereby we come to an informed decision regarding the appropriate course of action to be taken in a particular situation, or in deciding what is the correct or most advantageous choice to be made in any given circumstance. I believe it to be related to moral conversion or the pursuit of goodness in the same manner in which logical reasoning can be said to be related to cognitive conversion or the ongoing search for truth.

Balance scales are an excellent metaphor for this type of reasoning as they portray the importance of the precision, accuracy and exactness which analogical thinkers bring to the process of discernment when making a decision or judgement, and finally a choice.

The enneagram suggests that gut centred personalities experience life through the senses of hearing and smelling, both of which are related to their instinct for survival. Because hearing and smelling have always been recognised as the most primitive senses and nature's first line of defence, being 'noise and smell sensitive' can be great aids to the avoidance of whatever may endanger life. Just as logical thinkers depend on sight as their main contact with reality, analogical thinkers depend on hearing, and it is the freedom to listen and accept with trust the judgements of others which eventually will save them from their compulsive need to weigh and measure everything to their own satisfaction.

According to the enneagram the analogical thinker's focal point in the physiological system is the gut, which is the physical centre of gravity and balance in the human body. The location of the body's centre of gravity in the gut is said to gift those who live preferentially from this centre with a facility for balance and equilibrium in whatever may engage their attention. Be it sport, music, finance or politics which attract them, they not only strive to think in a balanced and organised way but also to move and act with grace and elegance.

This gift of balance and discernment is evident in the intellectual sphere by the patient and careful way in which analogical thinkers weigh up the pros and cons when making a decision, even though they may eventually decide, against all rationale, to follow their gut instinct. They also seem to have a natural facility for spiritual discernment and for good judgement in relation to life, and are said to have a natural facility for counselling. Some of my gut centred friends have told me that they find it comparatively easy to give guidance and advice to others but not always sure what is best for themselves.

That these same individuals can be physically clumsy and appear to lack balance and equilibrium away from the sports field or dance floor, is also worthy of note. 'Thinking', it would appear, can seriously hinder the movements or decisions of analogical thinkers and cause them to 'trip'. Gut reactions are, therefore, an important element of their ability to avoid inconsistency or inaccuracy in their movements, both physical and mental, and they are often at their best when following their natural gut instincts and reactions.

Though the strength and focus of analogical reasoning is balance and equilibrium, taken to extremes this can lead to an unrealistic demand for perfection and exactitude – which is anything but balanced. A desire for the best can make analogical thinkers compulsively critical, demanding or judgmental of everything and everyone including themselves. It is difficult for them ever to be satisfied, and because of this they find it difficult to attribute praise or merit.

This exacting demand for balance by the analogical thinker can become a critical pursuit of perfection which effectively may prevent them from recognising or attaining wholeness, then in frustration at not attaining their goal they may become punitive, exacting and even more demanding. Examples of this are publicly available in the sports world, but as a natural pitfall of this approach to life and reasoning, this lack of balance is equally evident and rife in other professions, as can be seen in recent times in some of the very controversial judgements given in courts of law.

The proclivity for equality and balance which is characteristic of analogical thinking is often expressed in the social arena by interest in social justice and fair play. Equal rights; recognition of the special needs of different individuals and groups in relation to physical, educational, economic, political and cultural requirements; environmental issues; all of which relate to quality of life, will engage the interest and energies of gut centred personalities in a struggle to achieve an egalitarian society.

However, the preoccupation with equality may not always augur well for those who, for one reason or another, are considered to be outside the main stream of society, as such individuals or groups may be perceived as a threat or impediment to the achievement of the equality or 'perfection' being sought. Difference of culture, life-style, creed or race may then become the focus of negative concern, in such a way as to subvert human rights to an unrealistic and unattainable demand for conformity and uniformity. Just as logical thinkers can be dogmatic in their control of truth, analogical thinkers can become rigorously fundamental in their control of standards. Egalitarianism may then give way to the desire for meritocracy.

97

As the proverbial 'flies in the ointment' history has shown how elimination of the 'weak or faulty' in society may be chosen as the best way of containing the divergent influence from whichever source it may spring, as evidenced in this century by so called 'ethnic cleansing'. This is analogical reasoning gone haywire. Compulsed gut individuals or societies are nothing if not radical, but that the exaggerated bias of the 'purist' denies personal authenticity and lacks rational balance is often not recognised by those by whom it is fostered.

Another negative effect of the uncontrolled and unbalanced pursuit of perfection may lead to a 'tit-for-tat' mentality in opposition to others. On a recent visit to Northern Ireland I noticed that in some areas the curb stones had been painted red, white and blue, whilst in other areas they were painted green, white and gold. This was not the work of children playing games, but of adults engaged in serious political combat. It may not appear to others to be a logical approach to the recent political situation in Northern Ireland, but in gut terms it was both reasonable and just. At the level of curb stones political wrangling is perhaps something that could be tolerated, but, as we are well aware, it does not remain at this innocuous level.

In their desire to make good choices, analogical thinkers may become stymied by the amount of information they need to process. Instances of this may be noted when shopping with gut centred individuals who, in making a purchase, seem compelled to weigh and consider every aspect of the object they wish to acquire. Slowly and carefully they consider ever facet of the purchase in relation to design, colour, style, texture, price and any other pertinent factor, and then compare it to the variety of other options on offer.

As a mark of prudence in relation to the purchase of major items such as housing, furniture and transport, this may be recommended, but when analogical thinkers insist on bringing the same perspicacity to the purchase of a loaf of bread or pair of slippers, it is possible that others may consider them to be somewhat unbalanced. It is possible that the apparent need they have to evaluate and scrutinise every purchase they make is rooted in their need for excellence and certainty, and it is this need for perfection in whatever they do which deprives them of the freedom and life they so eagerly and earnestly desire. Their dilemma is in needing to be well informed before making a decision, whilst knowing from experience that they make their best decisions by 'instinct'. Often they end up by not trusting their own decisions and consequently, without reason, may not trust the judgements of others.

In their reluctance to make what could prove to be a 'bad' decision or commitment, gut personalities appear to possess an almost compulsive need to constantly change the 'goal posts'. Their standards and requirements become increasingly more refined and composed until finally, and with some reluctance, they cast the die and make a choice.

Agility, suppleness and adaptability are important aspects of balanced judgement. The obsessively critical attitude to life that is portrayed by the compulsive gut personality was frequently condemned by Christ who, in response to the Pharisee's preoccupation with the minutia of the law, said:

'Woe to you, teachers of the law and Pharisees, you hypocrites.
You give a tenth of your spices, mint, dill and cumin.
But you have neglected the more important matters of the law,
justice, mercy and faithfulness' (Lk 11:46).

Thus, taken to extremes, rigorous pursuit of justice may become a yoke of slavery. By comparison, Jesus tells us of the life and liberty to be gained by accepting his yoke of love, which is for the meek and humble of heart.

Where, we may ask, do gut personalities find the solution to this deep and destructive dilemma with which they seem to have been saddled by nature? As has been suggested above, at some level their reasoning fails them, to the extent that, though they are gifted with the capacity for discernment and balanced judgement, they also appear to have a warped sense of perfection which gives them an unbalanced view of reality and life. I believe that the solution is simply one of finding our centre of gravity. Let me explain.

From the exploration of space which we have been privileged to observe second hand, so to speak, we know that nothing can be weighed in space. That is to say, in the absence of gravity, everything is weightless. I believe that the same principle applies to our capacity for judgement and discernment, and that in the absence of gravity no balanced judgement can be made. In other words, the attempt to balance anything, or to arrive at a judgement, decision or choice without first being earthed, is just not possible, for without gravity our judgements will lack 'value, power and merit' which is the Biblical meaning of weight. In making a judgement or discerning a choice, the first principle to be established is, therefore, where or what is our centre of gravity. This can be very problematic for analogical thinkers who, as stated earlier, can enter into all manner of contortion to avoid making a decision and seem to have an almost compulsive need to continually change the 'goal posts', i.e. to live without gravity. Only in the establishment of a centre of gravity do we become free to choose, do we become free to live.

Because life itself, and abundance of life, is the desire of analogical thinkers, this is what they and all of us are offered in moral conversion. Jesus proclaimed and promised that he had been sent by the Father to give us eternal life,

'Yes, God loved the world so much
that he gave his only Son,
so that everyone who believes in him may not be lost
but may have eternal life' (Jn 3:16).

This promise and hope of eternal life given to us by Jesus is, I believe, the 'centre of gravity' that validates all our judgements, decisions and choices in this life.

If our ultimate desire is firmly rooted in the hope of eternal life, all our decisions and choices can be effectively weighed and valued. No longer are we in the position of Topol trying to balance the pros and cons of choice in our hands and finding that we have run out of hands. Instead of trying to weigh the pros and cons against each other in a relentless, time-consuming balancing act, we now weigh each of them in relation to God's eternal desire for us, and make our decision accordingly. Making the decision that leads to life may not always be easy but will always free and liberate us from the stalemate and paralysis of procrastination.

To live with hope and to be motivated by promise is very difficult for those who by nature demand certainty. Just as it is difficult for head personalities to live with faith in the absence of sight, so, too, is it difficult for gut individuals to live with hope in the absence of certainty, but there is no other way for those who choose God.

The special grace that comes to us in moral conversion, which is to live continually in the discernment and following of God's will, is facilitated for us by God's gift to us of evangelical obedience. By listening attentively to God's word we are empowered to discern his will for us and for our world. The Latin verb audire captures the special sense of 'listening actively' which characterises evangelical obedience, and is the special faculty and prerogative given to those who actively seek to know and do God's will. This, I may say, is the difference between mere analogical reasoning, and the grace of discernment. Reasoning provides us with information, but discernment provides us with counsel and motivation. We pray not to be deaf. One final word; to live with hope is to live with rainbows.

SYMBOLS OF ANALOGICAL REASONING

The purpose of analogical thinking is to weigh the information that will validate or 'ground' a judgement or decision.

By a process of discernment leading to understanding it seeks to arrive at a balanced judgement that will ensure certainty, stability and freedom.

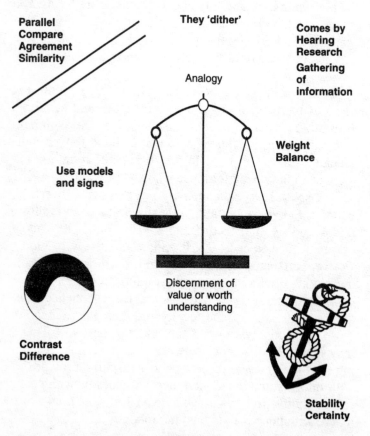

Parallel
Compare
Agreement
Similarity

They 'dither'

Comes by
Hearing
Research

Gathering
of
information

Analogy

Weight
Balance

Use models
and signs

Discernment of
value or worth
understanding

Contrast
Difference

Stability
Certainty

Generally speaking analogical reasoning is balanced and stable, but used defensively or negatively it can become judgemental, erratic and unreliable.

The gift of understanding
and counsel

Before Jesus ascended to heaven he promised his apostles that he would send them the Holy Spirit to remind them of all that he himself had taught them during his stay on earth. By the gifts of understanding and counsel this promise of Jesus is fulfilled and the Holy Spirit is given to us as teacher, guide and counsellor in order that our minds will be opened to understand and our hearts opened to hear the word of God.

To know the truths of faith is important, but to submit our conduct to the scrutiny of these truths so that our conduct is influenced and regulated by them, we need the gift of understanding. Until the knowledge of our faith is realised in practise we cannot be said to be living a Christian life and it is the gift of understanding which enables us to transform knowledge of faith to practise of religion. By this gift we penetrate the essential 'worth' of God and in the understanding of our own relative unworthiness we bow down in adoration and worship.

By the gift of counsel the Holy Spirit takes over the practical direction of our lives, and teaches us the way of life that conforms to our understanding and appreciation of the Divine goodness. By activating within us the grace of docility to God's word, the gift of counsel informs our faculty of discernment in relation to goodness, and urges us to make the choices that lead to life and freedom. In other words, by listening to God's word and being attentive to his counsel, we are able to discern his will in our regard.

The attempt to achieve greatness or goodness by one's own efforts or merits is, as we have seen in previous chapters, to misunderstand or negate the nature of morality or goodness. By the gift of understanding, our intellect is enlightened in regard to the intrinsic goodness of God and to the essential nature of goodness. This understanding makes it possible for us to comprehend that goodness is not something we are able to achieve by our own merits, but a quality that is gifted to us by God and is share in his own Divine life and goodness. It opens our hearts to the realisation of God's plan in our regard.

Attentiveness to listen, facility to hear, and courage to conform our lives to the example of Jesus, is the special grace given to us by the gifts of counsel and fortitude. The gift of counsel enables us to discern goodness and the gift of fortitude strengthens our desire and will to pursue it with generosity and courage. These gifts direct our moral lives by giving us a listening ear with which to apprehend, and the necessary courage to follow the discerned will of God in our regard. In other words, obedience to God's word, made known to us by the inspiration of the Holy Spirit, is the royal road to goodness, and to union with God.

The word that God speaks to us, in all the eventualities of life, is compassion. When God listens to us in our misery and need he listens with compassion, and when we listen to him his message is – be compassionate. God lives by compassion, he saves by compassion and rules by compassion. Compassion is the measuring rod of his strength, his power, his goodness and his glory; and we, who are created in God's image and likeness, have no other access to life, power and glory than that of compassion. In the words of Henri-Dominique Lacordaire,

'It is not genius, nor glory, nor love that reflects the greatness of the human soul, it is kindness.'

It is unfortunate that in today's society the very words used to express goodness and compassion such as tenderness, pity and mercy, have been debased and misinterpreted to express weakness and inadequacy rather than convey the idea of 'power and glory'. By the gift of understanding we come to know the true meaning of glory and realise that to live compassionately is to live with strength, power and honour; it is to live with justice and peace; with righteousness and pardon. It is to live, after the example of Jesus, as sons and daughters of a compassionate Father, and so attain the goal and grace of moral conversion.

In the process of analogical reason, people arrive at a decision concerning the qualities of goodness in relation to making the best choice available. Because of the skill which analogical thinkers have for debating, they are frequently less likely than others to be open to opinions and judgements contrary to their own. They tend to be very secure in their own ability to arrive at a balanced judgement and for this reason may be reluctant to 'give ears' to others.

The 'I know best' attitude with which we are all afflicted to a greater or lesser degree, may prevent our paying attention, not only to others, but also to the word of God and to the counsels of the Holy Spirit. Should this happen we cut ourselves off from the one certain route to goodness and life, and to the best of all possible choices, and no amount of discernment at the intellectual level regarding comparative worth will adequately substitute for the loss.

When we have 'ears to hear' the gift of counsel informs our understanding and leads us by way of obedience to participate in the salvation and life of the world. To listen to the word of God and be schooled in his message of love and compassion is, I believe, the gift of evangelical obedience, by which our wills are united to the will of God, and we are conformed to the likeness of Jesus.

'Blessed by the God and Father of our Lord Jesus Christ,
a gentle Father and the God of all consolations,
who comforts us in all our sorrows,
so that we can offer others, in their sorrows,
the consolations that we have received from God
    ourselves' (2 Co 1:3,4).

Charity

On one occasion I was visiting a friend whose youngest child Richard was just two years old. As we sat talking Richard came into the room and, making himself comfortable on his mother's lap, settled down for a nap. Waking up a short time later he seemed content to sit and listen until finally reaching out to touch his mother's cheek he said 'Mama, I can feel our hearts talking to each other'.

The theological virtue of charity which is a participation in Divine love makes it possible for us to speak to God in a similar heart to heart manner, in the way in which Richard conversed with his mother. This, in religious conversion is known as contemplation. The heart, universally recognised as the symbol of love, is considered in Christian theology to be the centre of our spirituality because, in the absence of love, it is impossible to be in relationship with God, self or others.

By the theological virtue of charity we love and delight in God for himself alone, with no ulterior or selfish motive. The love that is poured into our hearts by the kindness and grace of God enables us to love God with the love and affection that is the mark of God's own Trinitarian life where each of the Divine persons delights and glories in the other. By virtue of charity we love God for himself alone because of his beauty, truth, goodness and love, with no desire or wish for recompense or reward. By a love that is free from all personal interest and desire for gain, we witness to the presence and love of God in the world, and so become channels of that love to others. Only by sharing in the love of the triune God through the theological gift of charity does this quality of disinterested commitment become a possibility.

In the Gospel Jesus presents to us his heart as a model of the gentleness and humility which characterises the love of those who seek God in this selfless manner,

'... learn of me because I am
gentle and humble of heart
and you will find rest for your souls' (Mt 11:29).

Gentleness and humility are not particularly easy virtues to cultivate, but when the heart is captivated by Divine love they are effective signs of our 'being in love'. In his eulogy to love St Paul presents a formidable array of virtues that are characteristic of love, suggesting that love is not for the selfish or faint hearted (cf 2 Co 13). In truth the effect of love is to purify the heart from pride and all self-seeking, and to dispossess oneself for the sake of the other.

Because nothing we do can add to God's own intrinsic joy and happiness, no matter how ardently we wish to respond to God's love by loving him in return our response will always be weak and inadequate. Our love can, however, materially affect the lives of others, and it is by becoming channels of God's love for others that we give expression to the love we profess for God. As St John tells us, it is by loving those whom we see, that we give expression to our love for the God whom we do not see (cf Jn 4:20). As a participation in Divine love, the love we have for others must, of necessity, transcend all barriers of race, culture, creed and gender. Love is the only bond that can effectively unite the world.

In honouring the Heart of Jesus, who is the 'king and centre' of all hearts we recognise and pay homage to the love of God made known to us in the life and sufferings of Christ. In his epistle to the Romans St Paul tells us that,

'Christ died for us while we were yet sinners, and
that is God's own proof of his love towards us.'
(Rm 5:8)

This text teaches us that the measure of God's love for us is that it is unconditional, and operative even when least deserved. St John tells us that the love God has for us is, at once, the source and motivation of our love for each other. It is difficult to eliminate from our lives all trace of selfishness in order to love unreservedly with no conditions attached, but the theological gift of charity, which is a participation in God's own love, makes it possible for us to do so.

Constancy is another characteristic of Divine love which is a recurring theme of the Bible and God never tires of assuring us through the mouths of the prophets that,

'I have loved you with an everlasting love,
so am I constant in my affection for you' (Jer 31:40).

It is said of Aldous Huxley that he professed not to believe in everlasting life until the death of his wife. With her demise he came to the realisation that death has no power to destroy love and experienced himself as possessing an attribute that had eternal dimensions, and knew that he was destined to live for ever. Christian theology tells us that love is the essential ingredient of eternal life and that the love we have known and shared on earth will come to its perfection when we enjoy the beatific vision of God in heaven.

The creative force of love is another of its most celebrated and recognised characteristics and is manifested in the power of love to change and transform us in mind, soul and body. As the unique source of creative transformation love has no equal. To be the focus of someone's love and desire has a way of transforming us that gives us a genuine insight into our own value and worth by revealing to us our own inadequacy as a worthy recipient of love. 'Who could love me?' we ask ourselves in startled self-awareness and disbelief. The initial effect of realising oneself to be the object of love may lead to a sense of salutary unworthiness, self-doubt and discontent. Only when we understand the gratuitous and self-denying nature of love are we free to open ourselves to its creative and transforming effect.

It is by love that we are nurtured and sustained in the life of grace to which we are called by the grace of conversion,

'I will put respect for me into their hearts
so that they turn from me no more' (Jer 32:40).

As mentioned in previous chapters, though it is possible to profess faith and hope in the absence of love, without love it is impossible to be in a relationship of friendship with God. Just as the heart maintains the well-being of the body by circulating the life-giving blood to all its parts, so love is the vital ingredient that facilitates the flow of life from God to the world. God will never block the flow of his love to us, but it is possible that without the help of grace, we may impede the reception of his love.

The greatness of God's love for us can never be fully appreciated or understood. In fact, no true love can ever by fully expressed or comprehended because it has a Divine and eternal quality that knows no boundaries. In one of the most beautiful prayers of the bible Paul prays that,

'...you will, with all the saints, have strength to grasp the breadth and the length, the height and the depth of God's love' (Eph 3:18).

According to biblical commentary God's love for us in Christ, 'in breadth is boundless, in length is endless, in depth is fathomless or exhaustless, and in height is measureless' (cf *The Companion Bible*, p. 1765). The wonder is that, through the theological virtue of charity, we are empowered to participate in this most wonderful gift of Divine and Infinite love.

Affective conversion

To be in love is to desire union with the beloved by a total surrender and mutual gift of self to the other. In the reciprocity of the giving love becomes the most compelling and creative force of self-transcendence available to humankind.

All true love is a participation in Divine Love and to be dominated by love to the extent that all our thoughts, desires and actions begin and end in love is the ultimate goal of religious conversion. In order for this to be possible we are offered, in affective conversion, the gift of a new heart that enables us to enter into a relationship of intimate union and love with God. Such a relationship could never have been imagined or contemplated if it had not been revealed to us by God himself in the person of his son, Jesus, when he said:

> 'If anyone loves me he will keep my word,
> and my Father will love him, and we shall come to him
> and make our home with him' (Jn 14:23).

The essence of love, both human and divine is to share all that we possess, all that we desire and all that we are or may become, with the one we love.

The evangelical counsels of perfection known as poverty, obedience and chastity are I believe the means by which we attain this degree of union in our relationship with God. By the practise of these counsels we dedicate our goods to the service of God, conform our desires to the will of God, and treat with respect and love all those with whom we share life's journey. Together, the practise of these counsels is the means by which our love for God is expressed and becomes incarnate in our love for others.

Because poverty, obedience and chastity are the subject of the vows taken by members of religious orders, it may at times be supposed that these three evangelical virtues pertain exclusively to that particular vocation or way of life. They have, however, always been recognised in Christian spirituality as the way to perfect love of God for all Christians and are I believe an extension of Faith, Hope and Charity.

Like faith, the practise of voluntary poverty is rooted in God's fidelity and providential love. By poverty we free ourselves from whatever material considerations hinder our acceptance of God's invitation to become a disciple of Christ. Discipleship implies the willingness to follow and we cannot follow or travel in faith if burdened by excessive baggage.

Like hope, obedience is rooted in the power of God to save us from all harm and ultimately from death. Obedience is the acknowledgement and acceptance of our own innate weakness and vulnerability and our need for a saviour. Disobedience to God's word is an attempt to wrest power and save ourselves. By obedience we surrender ourselves to the compassionate and saving activity of God in our lives.

Like charity, chastity promotes unity and community, holiness and love. By chastity we recognise and acknowledge each one's unique and personal identity, and reverence the presence of God in each one. This is the basis of Christian community, and of our coming to wholeness in Christ.

By regulating our use of material goods, the practise of voluntary poverty recognises the rights of others to share in the wealth of the world. By obedience to the word of God we become empowered with the freedom 'wherewith Christ has made us free' (Gal 5:1). By chastity we conduct all our relationships with reverence and respect for the integrity of each individual person. Chastity is not about celibacy or about being married or unmarried, but about God's prior

111

claim to each and every person as his unique and loved creation and is a refusal to enter into abusive or destructive inter-personal relationships.

No one ever embraces love joyfully or with alacrity. Love is a dying to self and all self-seeking and, like dying, it is resisted, albeit weakly or fitfully, though sometimes strongly and enduringly. As the supreme sacrifice of self to or for another, love, which may initially start as a strong and compelling emotion, can only be sustained and nurtured by a deliberate act of the will. To accept the gift of a new heart in religious conversion implies the willingness to abandon oneself to God's loving providence, to surrender oneself to God's will, and to dedicate one's whole being and undivided heart to the honour and glory of God.

The pattern of 'on again, off again' relationship which is so characteristic of young lovers is sometimes experienced in our relationship with God when we are in the 'throes' of affective conversion. To be drawn into the magnetic field of love, whether human or Divine is to be exposed to a veritable vortex of emotions which can excite and liberate, compel and endanger, attract and repulse, all at the same time.

Affective conversion can be a time of intense inner struggle, of giving and retracting, of submission and rebellion, of willingness and resistance. It can be, in fact, an ecstatic experience of heaven or a bruising skirmish with hell. What we are struggling for is variously experienced as an effort to maintain personal identity and individuality, or the freedom to be ourselves. In love we resist becoming dependent on the presence, attention and love of another whilst experiencing ourselves to be irresistibly drawn to capitulate to their every desire and expectation. When the attraction is towards God, the struggle may become even more pronounced.

Paradoxically the surrender of self in love is not to relinquish ourselves but to attain the highest fulfilment of self through union with the Divine. Only when we are united to God in love are we capable of recognising and claiming our own unique identity because not until we see ourselves reflected in the beauty of God's love can we come to an understanding and acceptance of who we truly are.

In the process of religious conversion, in order to ensure our freedom of choice in responding to his love, God will at times appear to withdraw the sensible consolations of his presence but always remain within calling distance, even though hidden.

The fact is, the closer God is to us, the more immediate his presence, the more difficult it often is to discover him. Our situation might be compared to that of motorists who travel rapidly and with confidence to their destination along the motorway, but become confused and less certain of their bearings when they enter the labyrinth of streets which constitute the town. We may travel for years with our sight firmly set on God as our one and only destination and fail to recognise his presence when it is most immediate and imminent.

In Ignation spirituality affective conversion is the time when we are exposed to our 'sin', by God in love. Just as the effect of human love is to make us aware of our innate blemishes, so the effect of Divine Love is to draw attention to our sin. The Divine purpose in exposing us to our sin is in order that we may repent, be forgiven and share in the holiness of God. For everyone, this confrontation with sin can appear to be a struggle for life and survival. In process it can endure over a number of years but not always with the same intensity, as it is a process which has its 'spurts and plateaux' like any other growth.

To become 'dominated by love' is, according to Bernard Lonergan, the specific gift and grace of religious conversion. To be dominated by anything other than love, is to submit to being controlled by an external force which enslaves rather than liberates us.

The enneagram indicates that each of the centres or triads is dominated by a force or energy which is sought and adopted as the means of securing or achieving personal freedom and social harmony, and this dictates their manner of relating to others.

In affective conversion we are offered the 'freedom of the children of God' which is to be controlled or dominated by love.

By uniting us to God and others, love is the pre-eminent grace which makes it possible for us to enjoy heaven even here on earth, by creating the loving conditions in society whereby the Kingdom of God may flourish. When love dominates we recognise ourselves to be, and are identified as, unique individuals with rights and responsibilities bound to others in perfect unity and harmony with and by the Will of the Father. In the absence of love the opposite prevails, and chaos reigns.

Affective conversion is about love, and love never comes to us as an unadulterated pleasure, always there will be discouragement, uncertainty and disappointment even if these arise from our own inability to be totally committed to the relationship. The Peruvians say that:

'When God wants to enlarge a heart
he begins by breaking it' (cf Lk 2:35).

In each of the three centres, head, gut and heart, affective conversion can be a particularly distressing and painful experience, because it is a time when we struggle to free ourselves from our self-chosen slavery to whatever force is dominant in our life, and strive to respond to God's invitation to embrace life and love.

Affective conversion in the head centre

According to the enneagram head centred personalities are dominated by authority, and hold in high esteem and honour those who have been invested with authority. This will naturally have an influence on all their inter-personal relationships.

114

It is important for persons in this triad to be seen to support authority and to be recognised and acknowledged as loyal and dependable employees or colleagues. This is the image they desire to project and promote of themselves. It can be difficult for them to be objective in their dealings with authority figures, and even to think independently of the stance adopted by their immediate superior. It is not to be wondered at, therefore, that those in authority, tend to surround themselves with this type of personality.

In its original and true meaning, 'authority' means to teach, but in its generally accepted definition it has come to mean the power or right to enforce obedience. By nature and grace, individuals in this centre have a great respect for education as the means by which an enlightened and harmonious society is established, and individuals are helped to achieve personal maturity, freedom and fulfilment. In furtherance of this they have a natural desire to help others, particularly the young, to 'see' or discover the path of enlightenment in relation to knowledge and truth, and to encourage them to forge new paths of exploration and discovery in their search for personal fulfilment and meaning. Their desire to teach and their respect for knowledge and truth are a valuable contribution to the establishment of a stable society in which individuals are nurtured in their physical, mental, emotional and spiritual development.

That is the theory of how authority is exercised, but in practise the situation may be different. In a compulsed state head personalities need to prove that they are right, and those of them who exercise authority may be tempted not to 'teach' but to 'rule'. When this situation prevails, authority may cease to be a talent exercised in the service of others and become a tool of oppression used against the interests of others.

The need that head centred personalities have for peace and security and their dependency on the directions of others may foster the exercise of an 'authority' that rules and dictates rather than that of a 'teaching' which instructs and liberates. If authority is not exercised in the service of individual freedom and the pursuit of truth, it needs to be challenged; and in such circumstances a healthy disregard for authority may be a saving grace.

From head centred friends of mine I have learned that in the 'throes' of affective conversion, head personalities may have an experience of desolation which is associated with darkness, confusion and loss of direction. Literally, they are deprived of authority on which they are so dependent and can no longer move with confidence and security. Lacking vision, the way ahead is obscured or alternatively they may be confused or dazzled by the bright and glaring lights of a spiritual 'spaghetti junction' from which all sign posts have been removed.

For many, in the initial stages, affective conversion can be a time of fear and emotional upheaval. Deprived of their security they experience a sense of panic and fear at finding themselves lost and abandoned. They no longer have any dependable structures on which to rely for support, no laws or rules they can latch on to for survival, no authority to show them the way. They are lost in a mist which apparently is all pervasive and from which there is no escape.

At this stage, doubt may enter their life, and they may even begin to question the existence of God, whilst clinging tenaciously to the truths of their faith. Gradually, but not without struggle, they accept the inevitable and surrender themselves to the darkness, some in desperation, others in hopeful abandonment to their hidden God. Then as they bow to the inevitable loss of God they slowly become aware that the darkness which envelopes them is the Shekinah or dark cloud of God's presence.

It would seem from this shared experience that in order to attain freedom head personalities have to be delivered from their dependency on external authority as their rule and guide. When they discover God in darkness their lives are radically changed, for in the embrace of God's immediate but hidden presence, they come to realise that during

116

the period of darkness they were lead and protected by Divine love to an experience of knowledge, truth and harmony that is beyond all imagining and desire.

They now realise that the absence of signposts was not a sign of their being lost, but of having reached that point of their journeying at which signposts are redundant. They have, in fact, arrived at the haven of truth, goodness and love.

This is the great truth that we come to in religious conversion. Our destination is God, who is Love, and when we allow God to take over the direction of our lives, making love its dominant and motivating force, we are brought into harmony with the universe and society in a way that could never by achieved by mere conformity to law, or authority. Head personalities now realise, with a continually growing awareness, that Love is the principle and foundation of harmonious living, and, as such, must supersede law as the dominant authority in their lives.

Affective conversion in the gut centre

Gut personalities are said by the enneagram to be dominated by power for, in their perception of reality it is the acquisition of power which will ensure their security and survival. Without power or energy we die, therefore, for people whose compulsion is not just survival or existence but life in all its fullness, access to power is paramount.

To enjoy the good life, to acquire not just the essentials but the 'niceties' of life is the dream of gut personalities. Their desire for life is not entirely selfish as, in their concern for human rights and human dignity, they appear to have a genuine desire that others too may enjoy the blessings of an abundant and fruitful life. Nevertheless, in the final analysis their own survival comes first, and to achieve this the acquisition and control of power is considered to be a basic necessity.

Paradoxically, in the interest of acquiring or sustaining

life, gut personalities often seem to embrace death and destruction, or to use energy in a destructive rather than in a creative manner. The mayhem of violence and destruction so characteristic of today's world as daily recorded by the media, is like so much of what appears on cinema – the portrayal of the violent abuse of power in the service of death rather than life. When power is no longer seen as a means but as an end in itself, it may be considered legitimate to destroy or kill others, and this by those who claim to be seeking life.

We all need power in order to live. Used creatively, energy nurtures and enriches life, used destructively it impoverishes and destroys life, and this is true not only in reference to power generating plants or national power grids, but to our own mortal supply of physical energy. We each have only a limited supply of power or energy, one day it will run out and we will die, but the use we have made of our energy will live on after us, either as a force for good or a force for evil. This is a salutary thought.

Health and strength, power and energy are important for gut centred personalities who abhor weakness in any form as a possible threat to life. They want to be recognised as strong and unemotional, brave and dependable, powerful and consistent. They are, by gift and talent, the natural leaders of society, having all the verve and energy that such a role demands. Given the opportunity they can lead others with courage and determination on the road to freedom. However, ambition can be a strong temptation for them, and when this predominates they no longer seek to lead but to control others, and perhaps, should others present a challenge to their leadership or power, even destroy them. When this happens they are no longer leaders but tyrants and despots.

Perhaps more than other types of personalities they have trouble with the experience of love which apparently calls them to surrender in submission to the charming power and magnetic attraction of another. The abdication of power or control is not something they willingly con-

118

cede. To be controlled, even by love, is a threatening experience for gut personalities.

Gut personalities who have shared with me their experience of affective conversion frequently use the language of power and submission when talking about the experience. All speak of it as initially being a life-threatening experience, in which they feel helpless and vulnerable. Just as head personalities appear to be robbed of authority at this crucial stage, gut personalities seem to be exposed by God to the experience of vulnerability and weakness. The thing we most abhor or fear is often the means chosen by God to lead us to love.

Whereas head centred individuals speak of losing direction and sight during this phase of conversion, gut personalities often experience the process as losing ground, of losing their balance, of being out of their depths. They no longer have any firm convictions on which to lean, no firm territory on which to stand, no sense of being earthed or rooted. Invariably they speak of it as falling or sinking, of being swamped or inundated, and at times of being trapped. Some experience it as being pursued or chased, crushed or defeated, and even of being devoured. In fact, they feel themselves to be powerless, weak and vulnerable.

On more than one occasion I have noted great similarities between Francis Thompson's 'Hound of Heaven', and the experience of gut personalities in the process of affective conversion. To be in the presence of a superior power may tempt them to despair, or perhaps even to presume that they can outwit God by ignoring his presence or running fast. If they are faithful to prayer, they eventually come to the realisation that though they may run and hide, they cannot escape the attention of God and wait with resignation perhaps in agreement with the Muslims that 'God is the final conqueror'.

St Peter walking on the water also comes to mind when listening to gut personalities, because it is precisely this type of experience they seem to endure.

Rather than a 'dark night' there is a very real sense in

which religious conversion for gut personalities is experienced as a rough and tempestuous sea. Nothing is certain or secure, everything is weak, fragile, defective or unbalanced. Eventually, when their energy is spent and their resistance wains, in surrender they call to God from the 'depths' and like Elijah discover that God is not in 'the storm', the earthquake or the fire, but in the sound of a gentle breeze' (cf 1 Kings 19:11).

Their discovery that God comes rushing to save and not, as they had feared, to conquer, is the moment of capitulation and surrender to love. In discovering God in 'gentleness' they are lead to know the power of God in love, the strength of God in weakness and the fortitude of God in vulnerability. In fact, it is alright to be weak, to be vulnerable and to be powerless, because these are the strength and measure of Divine love.

To discover that love is the greatest power of all and the only power capable of creating and maintaining life, is the effect of affective conversion in the gut centre. God always gives us what we want but in ways that are unimaginable.

Affective conversion in the heart centre

Heart centred individuals are said by the enneagram to be dominated by image as a means of securing friends. Because for them the purpose of life can only be understood and achieved by love, they have a need to be established in a close network of relationships. Friendship and contact with others is their security and their life, and this dependency on others makes them very sensitive and susceptible as to how others perceive and relate to them. An aspect of their domination by image is that they may feel compelled to adopt a 'role' as a means of relating to others, and so effectively place a barrier between themselves and others.

To be noticed and appreciated, consulted and listened to gives people in this group a sense of achievement and well-being, provided the attention they receive is affirmative and authentic. A problem for them is that they desire recognition and love so frantically that they cannot believe others are being genuine when it is offered. They can have so little confidence in their ability to attract love, that they may angle for compliments or attention with the same intensity with which head personalities angle for authority and gut centred persons attempt to gain power.

There is, however, another important dimension to the manner in which image is recognised as a key element in our search for identity. In his book 'The Human Animal' Desmond Morris has a chapter entitled 'Beyond Survival'. This chapter draws attention to the fact that in any civilisation, once survival is assured, the energy of the adult population is diverted to the pursuit of 'play' and the acquisition of 'culture'.

For example, though the first concern and need of an island people may be to construct boats with which to fish, once they have acquired skill and expertise in boat building and fishing they devote their excess energy to embellishing their boats with colourful designs. The care and artistry with which they construct and adorn their boats are a proclamation of who they see themselves to be and are a mark of personal identification and ownership.

Self-adornment in primitive societies or civilisations was a sign that the people had advanced beyond the stage of mere survival, and could devote their energies to what Desmond Morris refers to as 'adult play' or the pursuit of culture. He further suggests that this indicates a higher level of intelligence than that of mere survival as it presupposes the acquisition of skills, or the ability to reason how best to achieve results, with the consequent saving of energy.

We all need image and imagery. Without theatre, poetry and art our lives would be denuded. At one time or another we have probably all tried to image or emulate, portray or mirror someone other than ourselves. In fact, it may be that only in imagery can we truly express ourselves, or only in the symbolic that we can truly be ourselves.

I remember on one occasion talking to a banker whose hobby was theatre. Marvelling that anyone could have the dedication to spend hours practising to perfect a minor role in an amateur production I asked him to explain his interest. 'It's my life', he explained, 'what I do at the bank is the charade, the theatre is for real'.

There is, I think, a very clear distinction to be made between play acting, which fantasises life and may be an escape from reality, and theatre which symbolises reality and is a profound immersion into life. Heart personalities tend to live at the level of symbol, and are, I believe, more naturally sensitive to the inherent vicissitudes and anomalies of life than people in the other two centres. Their desire is to live with integrity and authenticity which at times can only be achieved by symbolic representation, but is negated by role play.

The desire they have for integrity will engage heart centred personalities in a continual struggle to express themselves with integrity. To be understood and accepted is vital to their survival, and is more important than love, in fact in their perception, it is the highest experience of love. In their desire for understanding heart people may experience great tension between overstating or exaggerating their 'truth' and the failure to encapsulate it with integrity. It is a dilemma with which they continually struggle.

It is because of their need to be understood by expressing the depth of their feelings that heart personalities resort to, what may invariably be experienced by others as exaggeration, fantasy, symbolism or plain unadorned lies. Part of heart conversion is to recognise and confront the difference between these, and to eliminate from their lives all that is deceit. Only then can they achieve that which they most desire, the integrity and simplicity of expression which are the hallmark of love, and of the undivided heart.

Heart centred individuals are often frustrated in their search for love for the simple reason that they see love solely as something to be received and not something to be given or shared. For this reason they need religious conversion.

Affective conversion for heart personalities is closely bound up with their need to be understood and to be in relationship and is frequently experienced as a withdrawal of friendship on the part of God. In describing the process heart people talk about feelings of isolation and abandonment by God. At times they experience themselves to be fragmented or shattered, and speak of being diminished, rejected or exposed. They may lack a sense of wholeness, and feel as though they have been blown asunder. To be annihilated would be merciful, what they cannot endure is to be rejected or disowned.

Worn out by the lack of contact, heart personalities may also describe or experience the process of affective conversion as one of dissipation and detachment, when interest waxes and wanes in an unprecedented and unpredictable manner but in an ever downward spiral of depression. Everything is in flux, life seems 'blah', and they gradually lose their 'savour' for all things spiritual.

When this happens they may consider themselves to be used or perhaps even abused by God, and desiring nothing more than an escape from the relationship, they try to lose 'touch' with God. However, not being able to endure the prospect of self-imposed separation, they put the onus on God to take the initiative and end the relationship, which he stubbornly refuses to do. Like Jeremiah, they may then be tempted to say:

'You have seduced me, Yahweh,
and I have let myself be seduced;
I used to say, 'I will not think about him,
I will not speak in his name any more'.
Then there seemed to be a fire burning in my heart,
imprisoned in my bones' (Jr 20:7,9).

In one sense this is the story of their lives. Heart centred personalities fear to be known, because 'if you know me you may not like me'. They want to touch and even be touched, but are fearful of being possessed. They want to

123

be in relationship, but do not want to be 'invaded' or lose their individuality. They seem to be a shambles of contradictions, and are accused of not knowing their own minds, appearing to demand affection, attention and love, and then withdrawing in apparent disdain when these are offered. They find it difficult to initiate a relationship for fear their intentions will be misunderstood or misrepresented, and are bewildered when others, out of respect for their evident desire for privacy, do not include them in the conversation. What a disaster!

Exposure is both their fear and their salvation, and it is this painful experience which prepares them for the grace of affective conversion. Once they have exhausted themselves on a 'merry-go-round' of evasive behaviour they arrive at that moment of utter exhaustion that exposes them to the reality and wonder of God's unconditional love. In the amazement of discovering themselves to be understood, loved and desired, they lose all fear of rejection, for the light of Divine Love reveals them to be made in 'the image and likeness' of God.

This is the realisation of their 'unique and separate' identity which can never again be denied or taken away from them, for it is God's gift to them of holiness, by which he names and claims them as his own. United in will by love, they are established in relationship by the gift of understanding and confirmed in integrity by the gift of wisdom. They have arrived at the haven of bliss where they know they belong.

In summary

Each person who is faithful to prayer and their relationship with God will, in their own way, in a place and at a time chosen and decided by God, experience the pain and the grace of affective conversion.

For head personalities the struggle may be experienced as a search for God who has clothed himself in darkness,

'LOVE, LOVE CHANGES EVERYTHING'
(*Andrew Lloyd-Webber*)

When LOVE is dominant in our lives it is the most creative and transforming force in the world.

According to the enneagram HEAD, GUT and HEART centred personalities are dominated respectively by *authority*, *power* and *image*.

Only when *authority*, *power* and *image* are founded and rooted in love and are directed towards *love* do they become a creative, life-giving source of unity in the community.

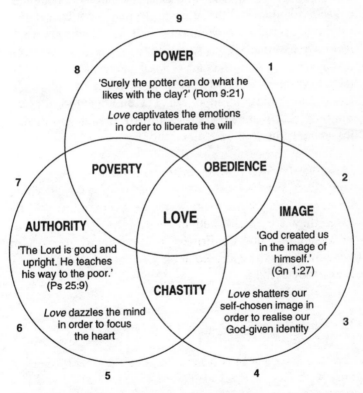

The practise of the evangelical counsels of *poverty, obedience* and *chastity* are the means by which we surrender all that we possess, desire and are to the domination of Divine love.

and is no longer available or dependable. They become confused and dismayed, until they realise that, in fact, they are enveloped in love.

Gut centred people often struggle, not with a hidden God, but with a God whom they perceive to be all too imminent, demanding, challenging and life threatening. Like Jacob they find themselves wrestling with God in an unequal combat from which they wish to escape. As their ambition for power wanes they discover themselves to be in the power of a God whose only strength is love.

Finally, in the same experience, heart individuals appear to encounter a God who denies their independence and individuality and threatens to destroy them by exposing their 'disguise' or shattering their image and the role they have assumed. In resistance they may attempt to shun God, but on hearing the call of their name they are motivated to surrender to God's presence which once and for all destroys their mask by love. This is the moment of discovering their own innate beauty and true identity, and the beginning of heaven here on earth.

Analytical reasoning

In processing their experience of reality, heart centred personalities are considered by the enneagram to be distinguished by their preferential use of analytical reasoning. By definition, analytical reasoning is lateral, diffuse and open-ended and can be markedly tangential, divergent and digressive. This type of reasoning, which can be circuitous and convoluted, would appear to pattern the functioning of the heart in circulating the blood, in other words their thinking appears to go 'round and round' in an all embracing circuit.

Like a spiral or helix, analytical reasoning may be compared to the winding of a coiled thread or the groove of a gramophone record, any point of which is related to and is in a direct line of contact with all other points.

A distinctive trait of analytical thinkers is their proclivity to move from one point to another in an unpredictable and, at times, apparently disconnected manner, along the circuit or line of reasoning being pursued. The ease with which such thinkers extrapolate information can be very confusing for those who are not familiar with their mode of thinking, and who are unable to forge connections with the same alacrity and accuracy.

For analytical thinkers every subject is extended by a network of relationships, and it is the discovery and investigation of these relationships which capture and hold their attention. For them, every idea may 'shoot or sprout' a prolific number of insights, each of which may be considered worthy of investigation. In their desire to understand more profoundly the subject being discussed, analytical thinkers are liable to take quantum leaps from one idea to another in the awareness that each is significantly related.

This gives them the facility to make valuable contributions to almost anything being discussed, be it only at the level of alerting others to ways in which the topic may be constructively and creatively extended.

Because they operate with a 'network' of ideas and concepts, it is feasible for analytical thinkers to join a discussion group or planning committee at any point in the proceedings and be immediately in 'touch' with whatever has already been discussed. Such thinking is often highly intuitive and inspirational, giving the analytical thinker access to knowledge which others do not perceive. Frequently such thinkers miss the 'obvious', but in turn are in touch with an inner reality hidden from others.

Analytical reasoning is facilitated for heart personalities by the high level of intuition with which they are often gifted, and it is this gift which enables them to be in touch with an inner reality which is unperceived by others. They often possess a very accurate sense of cause and effect, and know the probable outcome of decisions being considered before others perceive them. They can be quite intolerant of what they consider to be the frivolous arguments and debates of logical and analogical thinkers, which can appear to them to be so lacking in 'common' sense. For example they would have no time for the nonsense of the Pharisees of the Gospel story who tithed the dill.

Rather than 'facts' or 'information', analytical thinkers pursue 'understanding' and 'wisdom' as the gateway to truth. This they acquire by a process of breaking down into its component elements the composition of the subject or matter being considered. When these basic elements have been identified, the analytical thinker begins to trace or weave connections with numerous other subjects or topics. To those who do not naturally think in this way, this may appear to be unnecessarily complicated, but for the analytical thinker it is quite simply a matter of innate intuition. Those who query the validity of intuition as a means of acquiring truth should live for a time with someone who possesses this gift.

In addition to being highly intuitive, analytical thinkers are often original and inspirational. As mentioned previously, the enneagram suggests that nations as well as individuals have an enneagram number, and it has been suggested by some that as #4's in the enneagram, the Japanese and English belong to the heart centre. The creative ability of both these nations would appear to give some weight to this suggestion.

To be an analytical thinker can actually involve the experience of living ahead of one's time, because one is already in touch and familiar with ideas and concepts long before they are promoted or implemented.

If you are aware of being ill at ease in someone's company it may be that you are using different modes of reasoning, and so are unable to communicate. It seems to me that analytical thinking does not command the same respect accorded to the other two types discussed in earlier chapters. One reason for this may be that logical and analogical thinkers are threatened by analytical thinking, each for different reasons, and vice versa.

Logical thinkers require a structured, sequential and systematic mode of reasoning, and in their inability to follow the maze of connections being made by analytical thinkers, will accuse them of introducing 'red herrings'. Analogical thinkers are also unhappy with the discursive characteristic of analytical reasoning and may attempt to 'tether' them to their own precise mode of thinking.

Another reason why analytical thinking may not be fully appreciated is that such thinkers have a natural tendency to analyse everything and everyone, and what could be more distressing than to be the subject of a critical examination? To be with a compulsed analytical thinker is to be analysed, just as to be with a compulsed logical thinker is to be defined and to be with a compulsed analogical thinker is to be judged. The emphasis is on 'compulsed'. When people move away from their basic compulsion they are able to integrate their mode of reasoning and adapt to each type as the situation requires.

A third and final reason why analytical thinking may appear threatening, and one which may be more weighty than the others, is that there are possibly more female than male analytical thinkers, and more male than female logical thinkers. Along with many of my heart centred friends, I share the experience of my ideas initially being rejected by logical and analogical thinkers, who in general seem to require time to process them, and who will then, unblushingly, present them as their own. In my experience men are the most likely offenders in this matter.

As has been indicated above, the physiological focal point of analytical thinking, according to the enneagram, is the heart and circulatory system. By preference heart centred personalities experience life through the senses of touch and taste and, therefore, need to be 'in touch' in order to get the feeling of a substance of event, and 'to taste' in order to savour the richness of an experience. Contact is the means which enables analytical thinkers to understand, express concern, influence, effect and impress, each of which is an important element of relationship. By implication they must, of necessity, live in the present, as we cannot touch or taste whatever is past or future.

Michelangelo's painting of the Creation of Adam explores and expresses the mysterious power of 'touch' to bring to life. In being 'touched' by God, Adam is recognised and known by God, and it is in the experience of being 'known, loved, understood and accepted' that each of us is brought to life. The Biblical image of the potter is also a powerful symbol of our having been made and formed individually by the powerful and loving touch of God.

In all interpersonal relationships, physical touch is a delicate and sensitive issue. To touch someone can be a mark of love and respect, an expression of intimacy and admiration, or a recognition and appreciation of friendship. However, used negatively touch can be deceptive, manipulative, wounding, invasive and destructive of relationships.

Heart personalities are tactile by nature, and enjoy the feelings of intimacy that closeness imparts. Because of this they can be very sensitive in regard to touch and, in the presumption that others share their needs, may in fact be 'out of touch' with the legitimate expectations of others. This may leave them open to the criticism of insensitivity or over-familiarity, which they may experience as a form of rejection.

Part of the problem may stem from the fact that touch sensitive people, in line with their mode of reasoning, tend to have a very fluid concept of personal boundaries. That the extension of boundaries is a characteristic of analytical thinking does, I believe, have some bearing on their inter-personal relationships. The almost casual way in which heart personalities will touch others when engaged in conversation, or when passing them, for no particular purpose, can be offensive to others. They, themselves, do not give any weight to their action, and are often taken by surprise when others are offended by their action or interpret it as an invasion of privacy.

When entertaining friends, heart personalities like to create a comfortable and cosy ambience of warmth and welcome, which in male/female relationships may also be the cause of misunderstanding. Rightly or wrongly, it can happen that, irrespective of their intentions, they may un-wittingly give cause for apprehension in those they are desirous of befriending and so find themselves liable to censure, or to the embarrassment of being misunderstood and rejected. Similar to head and gut individuals, heart personalities appear to impede, by their own manner of reasoning, the thing they most desire to achieve, in their case, wholesome and happy relationships.

When closeness, friendship and intimacy are mutually sought, they can be a powerful means of fostering personal growth and self esteem, because relationships which recognise and honour the integrity of the individual, are an essential element of all human growth. The opposite effect prevails when an abusive act of violence or neglect denies

131

the integrity or invades the privacy of an individual. Therefore, if a person has difficulty in establishing good relationships their human development may be seriously impeded or even frustrated.

Any relationship which diminishes a person's image, integrity or self worth, may lead them to 'harden' the heart as a means of self protection. We sometimes speak derogatorily of people as being a 'soft touch' implying that they can easily be deceived or manipulated. Simply to be taken for granted can be another hurtful experience which, over a period of time, can have the effect of 'hardening' the heart. Others may harden their heart in a denial of friendship or in avoidance of responsibility. Whenever, or for whatever reason, the heart is hardened, the flow of love in the community is impeded.

Besides hardening of the heart, analytical thinkers can lose their 'taste' for the spiritual and develop an interest in the unsavoury. Reading and audio visual material which may be presented as innocuous, can, in fact, be a slow but deadly poison, causing them to become spiritually sluggish and inert. Relationships may then become unhealthy and even pathological. This is true, not only with regard to intimate, personal or sexual relationships, but to the whole range of interpersonal relationships in which we live out our lives. When we lose regard and respect for ourselves we lose respect and love for others, and all our relationships become tainted and rancid. When this happens we may be tempted to,

'put bitter for sweet and sweet for bitter' (Is 5:20).

Does analytical thinking have anything to do with conversion? I believe it does. Along with heart centred people we all need to be understood and to understand in order to enjoy life. To be established in a network of relationships is essential to our well being, because none of us can claim to be independent, even in relation to the most basic requirements of everyday living.

132

To survive and create a happy and peaceful social environment for our own and future generations, our relationships must be characterised by simplicity, integrity, truth and authenticity. If these traits do not permeate our personal and interpersonal relationships, if they are not basic ingredients of national and international commerce, politics and culture, then we will not be able to realise our full potential and happiness as human beings.

Analytical thinking leads us to discover the simplicity and integrity, the uniqueness, authenticity and unity that are the hallmark of all healthy and worthwhile relationships. The beauty of analytical thinking is that it exposes us to the innate simplicity of the universe and all that it holds. Everything is connected to everything else, everyone to everyone else and no one can survive alone, for,

'I say to you:
As long as someone suffers,
the rose cannot be lovely.
As long as someone looks at bread with envy,
wheat cannot sleep'. (Manuel Scorza, Peruvian Poet)

In affective conversion we receive the special grace of singleness of heart,

'I will give them a single heart' (Ez 11:19).

In Christian spirituality this is understood to mean an undivided heart, a heart free from duplicity, deceit and innuendoes, a heart that is characterised by simplicity, sincerity and peace, a heart that is in love with God. These virtues, which are the foundation and principle of healthy and life giving relationships, are the riches of Divine love which are imported to us by the gift of wisdom, and the grace of affective conversion.

SYMBOLS OF ANALYTICAL REASONING

The purpose of analytical reasoning is to understand the factors that validate and promote relationships.

By a process of breaking the whole into parts, analytical reasoning reveals the congruence that exists between separate entities, and so come to an understanding of the underlying principles governing relationships and unity.

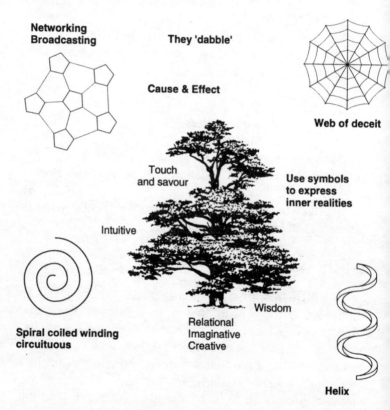

Generally speaking, analytical reasoning is imaginative, creative and original, used defensively it may insensitively expose or unmask the preferences of others and so become destructive of relationships.

Gifts of wisdom and contemplation

Like analytical reasoning, the gift of wisdom, which is activated in us by the theological virtue of charity, is about the nature and purpose of relationships. By the grace of this gift we come to know God, not just intellectually as the first cause and the principle of unity governing the world, but also in the Biblical sense of being in a personal relationship of intimate love. The gift of wisdom might therefore be said to transfer knowledge of God from the head to the heart in what Anthony de Mello refers to as 'heart knowing'.

By the gift of wisdom, which is the special grace of affective conversion, we are invited by God into a relationship of familial love which allows us to touch and savour the very life of the triune God. The words of the psalmist, 'Taste and see how good is the Lord' (Ps 34:8) reveal to us the profound and intimate nature of the union to which we are invited, and correlate to the manner in which heart centred individuals are said to process experience.

Because wisdom is gained by being in relationship with God, it is, therefore, unique and personal to each one, as no two relationships are identical. From the Wisdom books of the Bible we learn that,

'Even to think of her (wisdom) is understanding fully grown' (Ws 6:15).

Since the words wisdom, understanding and heart are used synonymously in the Bible, it may be supposed that to be fully grown in understanding is to be fully grown in love. The Bible also tells us that,

135

'She (wisdom) herself looks about,
looking for those who are worthy of her' (Ws 6:16).

Until wisdom seeks us out and fills us with the delight-
ful knowledge of God, all of our relationships will, of
necessity, be flawed. Only in the possession of wisdom,
which is the Divine principle and source of unity, are we
capable of being united to others in love. It is, therefore, by
the grace and power of this gift, freely offered to us by the
Holy Spirit, that we become established in a network of
harmonious and life giving relationships centred in God.

Because of the facility it gives us to penetrate and discern the appearances or false images under which reality
may be presented or disguised, the gift of wisdom extends
our capacity to initiate and sustain healthy and wholesome
relationships. By stripping away all that is superfluous or
merely cosmetic, wisdom reveals to us the very essence of
truth to be God, the fullness of whose love is the dynamic
force uniting and sustaining the universe. According to our
capacity for love and by virtue of wisdom we are united in
love, peace and joy with the whole of creation, and

'filled with the utter fullness of God' (Eph 3:19).

We are united in love, peace and joy with the whole of
creation.
On being touched or embraced by wisdom, we also discover ourselves stripped of whatever mask or persona may
have been our chosen disguise, and thus we both recognise
and realise our true identity. That such self knowledge is
given to us by God was acknowledged by Augustine of
Hippo when he said,

'What I know of myself
I know through the shining of your light.'

Only when we are held in the spotlight of God's love
can we know and accept ourselves as we truly are, 'warts

136

and all'. This, the beginning of true freedom, is the gateway to holiness, to that inner sanctuary of contemplation which is the state of perfect love.

Holiness, which in the Bible means 'to be separated' for God, is the grace by which we are chosen and entrusted by God with a unique and personal vocation, for which we are vested with a unique and personal identity. It refers to those things, places and events which God has chosen for his own purpose and design, and to those persons who he has consecrated by his love.

In his book 'The Sabbath', Abraham Joshua Heschel says that the first thing to be chosen and held holy and therefore separate by God is the Sabbath day. In creating time, God designated and chose one day which forever would be his, a sacred time of rest which we are asked to recognise as holy by setting it aside and separating it for God's purpose.

We also have been made holy by God's choice and separated for his own Divine purpose by virtue of baptism and it is this election by God which establishes our own unique identity and personal integrity. The only possible response to holiness or personal integrity whenever or wherever it is encountered, is respectful, reverent and silent contemplation, rooted in the recognition and joy of God's presence and love within the person.

I believe that contemplation or contemplative prayer is the grace by which we recognise and honour in ourselves, and others, the gift of 'holiness' that is a sign of God's election, a guarantee of God's love and the hallmark of God's ownership. In contemplation we honour the unique, wonderful and separate identity with which God graces each person and each act of his creation.

The experience of our own personal integrity, which comes to us as a revelation of Divine love, makes us sensitively aware of God's choice of or 'handling' of others. This truth, so profoundly experienced and taught by Julian of Norwich is the theme of a song by Jaime Rickert,

'There is nothing created in the universe,
Nothing great, nothing smaller than the finest grain of
    sand
That will spend a single moment of life
Without being held by its maker
In the hollow of His Hand
Be it something quite as simple as a hazel nut
He will hold it in the hollow of His Hand.'

To live in the respectful awareness of the 'integrity of being' of every person, animal, plant and humble 'hazel nut', loved and 'held in existence' by God, is the principle and foundation of unity, community and contemplative prayer. This is the fullness of wisdom by which we learn to relish the things of God and to savour the delights of God's creation.

Wisdom, which comes to fruition in contemplative prayer, is also, I believe, the principle and foundation of the evangelical gift of chastity. By the grace of contemplative prayer we live with a heightened awareness of the tender care with which God holds each and everyone of us 'in the hollow of his hand', and so imbues and permeates each of us with his presence. To recognise the awesome respect with which God loves and honours each inspiration of his love is to know and reverence their personal boundaries and to delight in their being a unique creation of God. Such knowledge will, of necessity, prevent our harbouring any desire to engage in, or promote, relationships which deny God's presence in the lives of ourselves or others.

To live contemplatively is to live in the conscious awareness of the unity of the universe and to pulsate in unison with the heartbeat of love, the heartbeat of Christ which circulates amongst us the Life and Spirit of God, and makes us partakers of his truth, his goodness, and his love. It is to recognise ourselves and others as belonging to the family of the triune God, partakers of his Divinity, and, under the inspiration of the Holy Spirit, to be united in praise and worship of the Father as Creator and Jesus as Lord. In this way we are drawn into the unifying and magnetic bond of harmony that unites us in mind, the shared commitment to goodness that unites us in soul, by the gift of a new heart which unites us in love.

According to the prophet, Isaiah,

'... those who hope in Yahweh
renew their strength, they put out wings like eagles,
they run and do not grow weary
they walk and never tire' (Is 40:31).

The Companion Bible notes in reference to this text that in the spiritual life,

'first we soar on wings, then we run, gradually we slow to a walk'.

Finally, we enter into that place of peace and rest which is God's gift to us of holiness and contemplation. It is a place reserved for the 'just' for those who have made compassion and pardon a way of life, for,

'This is Yahweh's gate which the just may enter.'

Within the gate all will be revealed and by the gift of wisdom we will know ourselves as we truly are, and reverence God as he truly is. God's gift to us of a new heart, which is the essence of conversion, will make this possible, and Jesus will say to us as he said to his disciples 'Happy are your eyes because they see, your ears because you hear' (Mt. 13:16). And in that day our hearts truly 'planted in love', will be

'...filled with the utter fullness of God' (Eph 3:19).

SYNOPSIS OF REASONING
IN RELATION TO CONVERSION

In order to be converted to truth, goodness and love, our reason has to be:

illuminated by faith
informed by hope, and
enkindled by charity

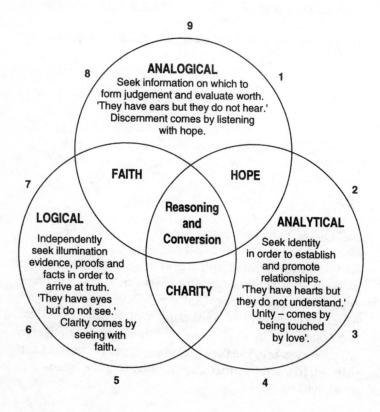

Reason illuminated by faith cures our blindness.
Reason informed by hope cures our deafness.
Reason enkindled by love cures our coldness.

Bibliography

Beesing, Nogosek and O'Leary: *The Enneagram*, Dimension Books Inc., Denville, New Jersey.

Fr Gabriel of St Mary Magdalen: *Divine Intimacy*, The Mercier Press, Cork, Ireland.

Gillie Oliver: *Ten Ways to Think Through Life*, Article in *The Independent*, May 1991.

Häring, Bernard: *The Characteristics of Conversion*, Herder & Herder, New York, 1966.

Heschel, Abraham Joshua: *The Sabbath*, Farrar, Straus and Giroux, New York.

Julian of Norwich: *A Shewing of God's Love*, Sheed & Ward, London.

Kelley, Sr Mary Helen: *The Human Trinity* (cassette tapes), Monastery of St Clare, Memphis, Tenn.

Edwards, Paul V.: *Today's World – The Image of the Trinity*, unpublished work.

Kung, Hans: *Christian Conversion: On Being a Christian*, Doubleday, Garden City, New York, 1976.

Lonergan, Bernard: *Method in Theology*, Herder & Herder, New York, 1979.

Morris, Desmond: *The Human Animal*, BBC Books.

Puhl, Louis J.: *Spiritual Exercises of St Ignatius*, The Newman Press, Westminster, Maryland, 1963.

Robbs, Paul V.: *Conversion as a Human Experience*, The American Assistancy Seminar on Jesuit Spirituality.

Rohr, Richard and Andreas Ebert: *Discovering the Enneagram*, Collins, Dove.

Sheets, John SJ: Unpublished material.

PAMELA HAYES

THE HEART IS A SACRED SPACE

A REFLECTION FOR 2000 A.D.

"The little space within the heart
is as great at the universe . . .
for the whole universe is in God
and God dwells within our heart.
                    (Chandogya Upanishad 8:1)

This reflection takes up a pilgrim stance in search of the space
of the heart, allowing the mystics and prophets to mingle with
psychotherapists and a whole variety of seekers along its
borderland.

What it discovers is that the heart is not only a psychological
sign of human vulnerability but a powerful symbol of a
theological reality. This is because we can see in the wounded
heart of Christ, an image of God that a world, aware of its own
brokenness, can receive. There, all at once, is the anguish of
humanity and the compassion of God loving us towards the
wholeness of being human. In Jesus, the heart is truly sacred.
But what is actual in him points towards a truth still to be
realised in every human being: that the heart is a sacred space.
The hope for all creation at the dawn of the twenty-first century
lies in rediscovering this truth.

PAMELA HAYES is a member of the Society of the Sacred
Heart. After many years in Higher Education lecturing in
Religious Studies, she is now involved in spiritual direction
and retreats and in forming others for this ministry.

ISBN 085439 493 1 – 208 pages